THE HEALTHY DIET CALORIE COUNTER

THE HEALTHY DIET CALORIE COUNTER

DUNCAN BAIRD PUBLISHERS

LONDON

REFERENCES

J. S. Bainbridge, *Diet for the Million* (Williams & Norgate Ltd, UK, 1926); R. Ballentine, *Diet & Nutrition – A Holistic Approach* (The Himalayan International Institute, US, 1982); H. G. Bieler, *Food Is Your Best Medicine* (Neville Spearman, UK, 1968); M. Bircher-Benner, *Food Science for All* (The C. W. Daniel Company, UK, 1939); W. Chan, J. Brown & D. H. Buss, *Miscellaneous Foods,* supplement to *McCance & Widdowson's The Composition of Foods* (Royal Society of Chemistry & MAFF, UK, 1994); H. Crawley, *Food Portion Sizes* (MAFF & HMSO, UK, 1992); S. Davies & A. Stewart, *Nutritional Medicine* (Pan Books, UK, 1987); Food Standards Agency, *McCance & Widdowson's The Composition of Foods,* 6th summary edition (Royal Society of Chemistry, UK, 2002); J. S. Garrow, W. P. T. James & A. Ralph, *Human Nutrition & Dietetics,* 10th edition (Churchill Livingstone, UK, 2000); B. Holland, et al, *Cereals & Cereal Products,* supplement to *McCance & Widdowson's The Composition of Foods* (Royal Society of Chemistry & MAFF, UK, 1988); B. Holland et al, *Fruits & Nuts,* supplement to *McCance & Widdowson's The Composition of Foods* (Royal Society of Chemistry & MAFF, UK, 1992); B. Holland et al, *Vegetables, Herbs & Spices,* supplement to *McCance & Widdowson's The Composition of Foods* (Royal Society of Chemistry & MAFF, UK, 1991); B. Holland et al, *Vegetable Dishes,* supplement to *McCance & Widdowson's The Composition of Foods* (Royal Society of Chemistry & MAFF, UK, 1992); R. E. Kowalski, *The 8-Week Cholesterol Cure* (Thorson, UK, 1990); J. G. G. Ledingham & D. A. Warrell (eds), *Concise Oxford Textbook of Medicine* (Oxford University Press, UK, 2000); T. Lobstein, *Fast Food Facts* (The London Food Commision, Camden Press, UK, 1988); The London Food Commission, *Food Adulteration and How to Beat It* (Unwin Hyman Ltd, UK, 1988); R. Mackarness, *Eat Fat and Grow Slim* (Fontana, UK, 1980); L. Mervyn, *The Dictionary of Minerals* (Thorsons, UK, 1985); L. Mervyn, *The Dictionary of Vitamins* (Thorsons, UK, 1984); J. L. Mount, *The Food and Health of Western Man* (Precision Press, UK, 1979); M. Murray & J. Pizzorno, *An Encyclopaedia of Natural Medicine* (Macdonald Optima, US, 1990); Parents for Safe Food, *Safe Food Handbook* (Ebury Press, 1990); A. A. Paul et al, *Amino Acids & Fatty Acids,* supplement to *McCance & Widdowson's The Composition of Foods* (Royal Society of Chemistry & MAFF, UK, 1992); W. A. Price, *Nutrition and Physical Degeneration* (The Price-Pottenger Nutrition Foundation, 1982); N. Rowley, *Basic Clinical Science* (Hodder & Stoughton, UK, 1994); J. Salmon, *Dietary Reference Values – A Guide* (Department of Health & HMSO, UK, 1991); S. Stender, J. Dyerberg, G. Hølmer, L. Ovesen & B. Sandstrøm, *Transfedtsyrernes Betydning for Sundheden* (Ernæringsrådet, Denmark, 1995); Weight Watchers, *1, 2, 3 Success* (Weight Watchers Ltd, UK, 1996); Weight Watchers, *Selection Guide – The A–Z of Selection Values* (Weight Watchers International Inc., UK, 1993); M. R. Werbach, *Nutritional Influences on Illness* (Thorsons, UK, 1989); World Cancer Research Fund in association with American Institute of Cancer Research, *Food Nutrition and the Prevention of Cancer – A Global Perspective* (American Institute for Cancer Research, USA, 1997); manufacturer and on-line data.

THE HEALTHY DIET CALORIE COUNTER Kirsten Hartvig

To Nic

Distributed in the USA and Canada by
Sterling Publishing Co., Inc.
387 Park Avenue South
New York, NY 10016-8810

This edition first published in the UK and
USA in 2004 by
Duncan Baird Publishers Ltd
Sixth Floor, Castle House
75–76 Wells Street, London W1T 3QH

Managing Editor: Julia Charles
Editors: Lucy Latchmore & James Hodgson
Managing Designer: Dan Sturges
Designer: Adelle Morris
Commissioned Photography: Matthew Ward

Library of Congress Cataloging-in-
Publication Data Available.
ISBN: 978-1-84483-319-1

10 9 8 7 6 5 4

Typeset in Frutiger
Color reproduction by Scanhouse, Malaysia
Printed and bound in China by Imago

For information about custom editions,
special sales, premium and corporate
purchases, please contact Sterling Special
Sales Department at 800-805-5489 or
specialsales@sterlingpub.com.

Publisher's Note: The information in this
book is intended only as a guide to following a healthy diet and is not meant as a
substitute for medical advice and treatment.
People with special dietary requirements of
any kind should consult appropriate medical
professionals before changing their diet.
The tables have been compiled using data
derived from a variety of sources including
manufacturer data. The literature sources
are listed together with other references on
page 4 (see opposite). Nutrient information
relating to Recommended Dietary
Allowances (RDA) has been calculated using
data from the USDA Food and Nutrition
Information Center. Some values have been
estimated based on similar foods.

ACKNOWLEDGMENTS
The author would like to thank Judy
Barratt, Geoffrey Cannon, Julia Charles,
Peter Firebrace, Peter Goldman, James
Hodgson, Lucy Latchmore, Jennifer
Maughan, Françoise Nassivet, Amanda
Preston, Nic Rowley, Bob Saxton, Joyce
Thomas, Linda Wilkinson, as well as all
those friends, colleagues, teachers, students
and clients who, knowingly or unknowingly,
have contributed to this book.

Contents

INTRODUCTION

Obesity is now a major threat to health. A staggering 61 per cent of American adults are overweight and obesity among children is increasing at an alarming rate. In most cases, the cause is simple—eating too many empty calories.

Empty calories are those that provide energy but little else of nutritional value. A chocolate bar, for example, may contain the same number of calories as an avocado, but it is not nearly as nutritious. If our food consists mainly of empty calories, we become both overweight and undernourished. The lack of vital nutrients in an empty-calorie diet lowers our resistance to disease and saps our stamina, making it difficult for the body to function properly.

This book is about quality calories—calories that come from foods that make you healthy. Whether you are trying to lose weight, or simply want to maintain your current weight in the healthiest possible way, meeting your daily calorie needs with quality calories automatically provides your body with all

the essential nutrients that it needs for good health. Quality calories are satisfying and nourishing, and make it easy to avoid over-eating. The more quality calories your diet contains, the less space there will be for empty calories.

High-protein diets and calorie counting can produce short-term weight reduction but sustainable weight loss involves improving the quality of each calorie you eat. High-protein diets work because the hunger center in the brain is sensitive to protein intake. However, the body uses protein primarily to create body structures, and only converts it into energy as a last resort. While a high-protein diet may be nourishing, protein overload can also cause health problems, and it is important for long-term health to eat foods that are well-balanced nutritionally. This does not mean boring meals and endless restrictions, it means enjoying more of the huge variety of inexpensive, widely available, energy-giving foods that are good for your body and good for you—foods rich in quality calories.

Part 1
CALORIES

Part 1 lays the foundation for the rest of this book. We start by exploring the background to calorie counting. We learn about the complex relationship between calories, food, and dieting, the role of appetite in regulating calorie intake, and how this mechanism can go wrong when we eat empty calories rather than quality calories. Next we are introduced to the nutrient tables. We discover the unique quality-calorie points system and the Quality Calorie Targets, and are guided through the process of using these tools to improve the nutritional quality of our diet. This is followed by a discussion of obesity and eating disorders. The section concludes with an explanation of the factors affecting our energy needs, and a step-by-step procedure for calculating our optimum calorie intake.

All about calories

CALORIES AND ENERGY

A calorie is a unit of heat energy, technically defined as "the energy needed to raise the temperature of one gram of water by one degree centigrade." In the body, the process of metabolism converts the calories contained in food into the energy we need to live. As even small amounts of food can contain thousands of calories of energy, it has become standard practice to express food energy in terms of kilocalories (where 1 kilocalorie = 1000 calories). One gram of carbohydrate provides just under four kilocalories of energy, one gram of protein provides four kilocalories, and fat provides nine kilocalories per gram. Fat is more "calorie-dense" than protein or carbohydrate because it is designed for the compact storage of energy.

It is possible, using charts and tables, to work out exactly how many calories we need for our age, height and activity level. However, the bottom line is simple: we need as many as we use. Children use calories for growth and are usually very active; but they are also small so they need fewer calories than adults overall. Older people are generally less active, so they

also need fewer calories. Pregnant and nursing mothers need more calories than average women because they have two mouths to feed. Overweight bodies use up more energy than non-overweight bodies, because they carry around extra weight.

If we eat more calories than we need, the extra energy released from food is converted into fat and stored for later use. If we don't use up our fat stores, we become overweight.

CALORIES AND APPETITE

The appetite is our natural in-built calorie counter that ensures we take in enough energy to fuel our daily activities. It makes us feel hungry when we need energy, and full when we've eaten enough. If we eat healthy food, the appetite does the calorie counting automatically. So, to take a major step toward maintaining a healthy weight, all we need to do is learn to pay attention to the signals that our bodies give us about what we need, rather than to what our eyes tell us we want.

EMPTY CALORIES VERSUS QUALITY CALORIES

For most of us, empty calories form a substantial part of our daily diet, making it hard for us to hear the quiet voice of healthy appetite (see box, opposite). Processed foods that combine carbohydrates with fats (cream cakes, for example) often produce feelings of immediate satisfaction when they are eaten. However, these feelings don't last because the calories are not accompanied by other nutrients that the body needs. As a result we are tempted to eat more empty calories and risk being trapped in a vicious circle of poor nutrition and increasing weight. More people pig out on chocolate cookies than on carrots, but even if you were to binge on carrots, the damage in terms of calories would be minimal: four chocolate cookies contain over 500 kilocalories, while four carrots contain just 35 kilocalories. Whether you are interested in slimming, or simply want to maintain a healthy weight, the vital step is to make the change from a calorie-dense, nutrient-deficient empty-calorie diet to a nutrient-rich, quality-calorie diet (see box, p.16).

Using the tables in Part 2 and Part 3, you will be able to identify foods with a high quality-calorie count (that is, foods

A typical empty-calorie diet

Breakfast	White buttered toast with jelly, coffee with milk and sugar
Morning snack	Candy bar, cup of coffee with milk and sugar
Lunch	Hamburger in a white bun with fries, a soda
Afternoon snack	Tea with milk and sugar, cake or cookies
Dinner	A few drinks followed by a processed food meal, with perhaps another few drinks

Although this diet provides plenty of calories, it is high in saturated fat, protein, and refined carbohydrate, and contains little useful nourishment. Excess saturated fat leads to the formation of dangerous fatty deposits in the blood vessels; excess protein causes bad breath and kidney problems; excess refined carbohydrates disrupt energy levels by upsetting blood-sugar balance; and calories derived from alcohol place strain on the liver.

with a high ratio of nutrients to calories). Eating more of these foods will improve the nutritional quality of your diet, and make it easier to keep up your energy levels with fewer calories overall. Simply by eating more quality calories, you will become healthier and find it easier to maintain an optimum weight in the long term.

In addition, you can use the information on vitamins, minerals, and trace elements contained in Part 3 to help you

Benefits of quality calories

Quality-calorie counting will help you to create a diet that is:

- high in fiber and complex carbohydrates
- high in polyunsaturates and essential fatty acids
- a rich and balanced source of protein and essential amino acids
- rich in all important minerals and trace elements
- high in natural antioxidants
- low in fat
- low in cholesterol
- low in saturated fats
- low in hydrogenated fats and trans fats
- low in refined sugar
- free from harmful artificial additives

monitor your intake of essential micronutrients, and to learn about their importance in the maintenance of health and the treatment of disease. The descriptions of each vitamin and mineral enable you to check whether you may be suffering from a deficiency, and you can then use the tables to increase your intake of particular micronutrients by modifying your diet instead of taking expensive supplements.

QUALITY-CALORIE COUNTING

The tables in Parts 2 and 3 have two special features to help you optimize the nutritional quality of your diet. First, calorie counts for different foods are listed "per average portion," which means you don't have to weigh or measure anything to work out your calorie intake. Second, each food is rated according to a unique quality-calorie points system, devised so that the most nutritious foods (those that are low in saturated fat, contain the right amount of protein, the right kind of sugar, and plenty of vitamins and minerals) receive the highest scores. Foods that score fewer than 50 points are the most unbalanced. This does not mean they have no nutritional value, but that the balance of nutrients they contain is far from ideal.

The proteins, carbohydrates, fats, fiber, vitamins, minerals, trace elements, and phytochemicals contained within the calories we eat give us energy to perform our daily tasks, and also help to prevent illness and promote healing. If you cut down on calories to lose weight, it is crucial that the food you eat has the right balance of nutrients. Choosing low-calorie foods with a high quality-calorie score ensures that your dietary needs are met while you are losing weight.

Follow these steps when using the Quality Calorie Guide to optimize your diet:

1 Use the calorie-intake tables on p.29 to work out how many calories you need each day based on your height, weight, sex, age, and activity level. Note down the figure.

2 Carry a notebook and pen with you everywhere for the next seven days. Each time you eat something, write it down. You don't have to weigh or measure anything, just make a note of how many portions you eat of which foods.

3 At the end of each day, use the tables to work out the total number of calories you have consumed that day by adding together the "kcals per portion" for each portion of food you have eaten. Note down the figure.

4 Next, add together the quality-calorie points for each portion of food you have eaten during the day. Divide this total by the number of portions you have eaten. This gives you your average quality-calorie score for the day. Note the figure.

5 At the end of the week, add all seven daily calorie-intake figures together, and divide the total by seven to find your average daily calorie intake. Compare this figure with your optimum calorie intake. If your average daily intake is more than 200 calories higher than the ideal, you risk gaining weight. If it is more than 200 calories below the ideal, your weight will tend to diminish over time.

6 Look back at your average quality-calorie scores for each day. The higher the daily score, the better the nutritional quality of your diet. A daily score of 50 or less suggests that your diet contains too many empty calories.

7 Use the results of your analysis together with the tables in Part 2 and Part 3 to optimize your calorie intake and increase your quality-calorie scores.

QUALITY CALORIE TARGETS

The tables also provide you with "Quality Calorie Targets" (QCTs) for the nutrients contained in different foods. These are worked out in accordance with the Food and Drug Administration (FDA) or World Health Organization (WHO) recommended daily amounts for women and show, at a glance, how close the nutrient content of a portion of a particular food is to the ideal. For proteins, carbohydrates, and fats, the QCTs indicate the ideal percentages of calories that should be derived from each of the three nutrients. You can compare these figures with the percentages given for particular foods to ensure that your diet provides a balanced source of calories.

For vitamins, minerals, trace elements, fiber, and essential fatty acids, the tables give the amount of each nutrient per portion of food in milligrams (mg) or micrograms (µg). By comparing these figures with the QCTs, you can work out how many portions you need to eat of particular foods to meet your daily requirements for each nutrient. (The body has a great capacity to store most nutrients, so you don't need to meet the target for every nutrient every day.) For example, suppose you wanted to optimize your zinc intake. Look at your diet record for day 1.

Using the tables in Part 3, note the zinc content of each portion of food eaten during the day. Add the figures together. If the total is less than the zinc QCT of 8 mg, you are not eating enough zinc. Repeat the exercise for days 2–7. If you find your zinc intake is consistently low, use the tables to find foods that are high in zinc, and include more of these in your diet.

OBESITY AND EATING DISORDERS

Obesity means excess body fat, and is usually caused by a mixture of poor eating habits, lack of health education, metabolic disorders, depression, genetic predisposition, and various social factors. It is also associated with a number of serious medical conditions, including coronary heart disease and cancer. One in six American children are overweight, and it is estimated that the obesity epidemic will cost Americans $260 billion a year in treatment by 2010.

People who are overweight clearly eat more calories than they use, and may have an altered sensitivity to hunger and fullness. This may be linked to reduced psychological resistance to sensory stimuli. Watching television is strongly associated with obesity because it provides strong sensory stimuli while promoting a sedentary lifestyle and lowering metabolic rate. This combination induces a trance-like state that makes it difficult to get up from the couch and do something active.

To complicate matters, fat cells seem to have been designed to make dieting difficult. If, as a result of calorie restriction, fat cells become smaller, they send increasingly powerful signals to the brain asking to be fed, resulting in an overpowering urge to eat. The larger the number of fat cells, the stronger the urge, which explains why when fat people (who have more fat cells) follow severe diets (which shrink their fat cells rapidly), they frequently suffer a "rebound" effect from dieting and put on more weight after the diet than they lost by following it. In fact, studies suggest that only five per cent of obese people are able to slim down to and maintain an "ideal" body weight in the long term, which explains the continued pro-liferation of books on diet and dieting. (A wise physician once said that the more treatments that are available for a disease, the less likely it is that any of them actually work.)

Maximizing sustainable weight loss involves losing weight slowly (between ½ lb and 1 lb a week). If you want to lose a pound a week, you must use up 500 calories more than you eat each day, which can be achieved by taking half an hour of aerobic exercise daily. A regular meal pattern (with little or no snacking) makes it easier to refrain from binge eating, and food containing plenty of fiber helps to keep the digestive system occupied. Also ensure that every calorie you eat is of the high nutritional quality to help your body resist cravings.

Recent research suggests that up to 30 per cent of obese people suffer from binge eating, a condition associated with eating disorders such as anorexia and bulimia nervosa. Binge eaters are more likely to be depressed and have anxiety disorders, such as panic attacks and post traumatic stress problems.

Both anorexics and bulimics have a distorted attitude to food. They suffer feelings of unworthiness and of being controlled, which are often rooted in rigid family patterns that can be hard to treat. Anorexia is characterized by persistent, active refusal of food, leading to profound weight loss. It is most common in young women, and leads to irregular or absent periods, strange eating habits, a disturbed body image, and sometimes depression. If untreated it can prove fatal.

Bulimia is closely related to anorexia, and bulimics are similarly obsessed with body weight and size. They use vomiting, laxatives, diuretics, dieting, fasting, or strenuous exercise to lose weight while at the same time indulging in repeated and uncontrollable binging.

All cases of binge eating, whether associated with obesity or eating disorders, should be treated medically, but there are simple self-help strategies which can alleviate some of the difficulties. Avoiding refined sugar, junk food, caffeine, alcohol, and recreational drugs helps to stabilize blood-sugar levels, improve metabolism and bring greater inner clarity. Eating regular meals containing foods high in calcium, magnesium, zinc, B-vitamins, and vitamin C also helps in this. Getting enough sleep, allowing time for creative expression and spending time outdoors assists in removing internal clutter.

How many calories do we need?

ENERGY NEEDS

A living body is rather like an internal combustion engine, burning fuel and oxygen to release energy, and giving off carbon dioxide and other waste products. This energy is used to maintain healthy functioning of the body and support activity. Not all the energy contained in food is available to the body. This is for two reasons: first, not all the food we eat is absorbed through the digestive tract (99 per cent of carbohydrate, 95 per cent of fat, and 92 per cent of protein is absorbed in fact); second, not all the protein we absorb is converted into energy—some of it is incorporated into the structure of body tissues.

Of the energy that is available, a great deal is used to maintain the basal metabolic rate (BMR). This is a measure of the energy needed to fuel all basic life functions while we are at rest. As well as the BMR, physical activity accounts for about 20 to 40 per cent of our energy use, with digestion, temperature regulation, and coping with the after-effects of physical exertion accounting for the rest.

There are a number of factors that cause variations in energy needs between individuals:

• **Body size** – The bigger you are, the more energy you will need to perform the same activities. Energy use is also affected by body composition. A well-muscled body burns more energy than a fat body (which explains why it is easier to keep a fit body in good shape).

• **Age** – Babies use a lot of energy to keep warm, and children and teenagers need extra energy to grow and fuel their often vigorous physical activities. As we get older, our metabolism slows down, our body tissues become more fatty, and we tend to become less active. Consequently, we need a lower intake of energy to maintain a healthy weight.

• **Sex** – Men generally need more calories than women because their body tissues contain less fat, their BMR is higher, and they are (on average) bigger. Pregnant women need extra energy to support the growth of the baby, and breastfeeding mothers require extra energy for producing milk.

- **Diet** – Overeating increases the BMR by five to ten per cent, while dieting reduces it by the same amount. Herein lies the paradox of weight loss: if you eat less to try to lose weight, your BMR drops, which means that your capacity to burn calories also diminishes. In effect, this means that dieting without an increase in physical activity is unlikely to produce sustainable weight loss. Aerobic exercise helps the process of weight reduction in three ways. First, it draws on energy stores while you are doing it, as well as during the following day when your body is recovering and readjusting. Second, exercise encourages the development of muscle, which raises the BMR. This means that you burn more calories at rest as well as when exercising. Third, exercise improves the circulation, enhances the absorption, digestion, and metabolism of food, and helps the body to rid itself of waste products.
- **Activity** – It is normal to eat more if you use a lot of energy for physical activity: athletes and heavy-manual workers have increased energy needs to match their energy output.
- **Climate** – Keeping the right body temperature consumes energy—shivering to keep warm and sweating to keep cool both use up extra calories.

- **Genetic factors** – These account for variations in BMR of up to ten per cent in people of the same age, sex, and body weight.
- **Hormonal state** – Thyroid over-activity increases energy expenditure, while thyroid under-activity reduces it. In women, the BMR is higher after ovulation. During pregnancy, the BMR falls initially, then increases as body weight increases.
- **Psychological state** – Anxiety and chronic stress increase energy expenditure.
- **Drugs** – Stimulants, such as nicotine and caffeine, increase energy expenditure. Amphetamines and other stimulants are sometimes used in treatment of obesity for this reason. Beta-blockers (often used in the treatment of hypertension and heart disease) decrease energy expenditure and can cause weight gain.
- **Disease** – Fevers, tumors, and the physiological problems caused by severe burns all increase the BMR.

BODY MASS INDEX (BMI)

The Body Mass Index (BMI) provides a simple method of checking whether your weight is right for your height and build.

1. Write down your weight in pounds (for example, 140).

2. Multiply this by 704 (140 x 704 = 98,560).

3. Measure your height in inches (for example, 66).

4. Multiply this number by itself (66 x 66 = 4356).

5. Divide the "weight number" by the "height number" (98,560 / 4356 = 22.62). In this example, 22.62 is your BMI.

Though simple to calculate, the BMI provides a powerful way of correlating weight to the likelihood of illness. Individuals with a high BMI are more likely to suffer from diabetes, hypertension and cardiovascular disease, as well as depression, respiratory disease, and ulcers.

The body mass index is interpreted as follows:

BMI		BMI	
under 20	= underweight	30–35	= obese
20–25	= healthy weight	over 35	= seriously obese
25–30	= overweight		

Optimium calorie-intake tables grouped according to age and sex

Children and young people (aged 1-18)

Average daily energy need (moderate activity)

AGE	BOYS	GIRLS
1–3 years	1250 kcal	1175 kcal
4–6 years	1700 kcal	1550 kcal
7–10 years	1975 kcal	1750 kcal
11–14 years	2225 kcal	1850 kcal
15–18 years	2750 kcal	2100 kcal

Adults

Average daily energy need (moderate activity)

AGE	MEN	WOMEN
19–59 years	2700 kcal	2050 kcal
60–75 years	2350 kcal	1900 kcal
75+ years	2100 kcal	1800 kcal

ADJUSTMENTS

• When involved in heavy activity or vigorous exercise add 500 kcal per day.
• If leading a sedentary lifestyle subtract 150 kcal per day.
• During pregnancy add 200 kcal per day during the last 3 months.
• While breastfeeding add 500 to 600 kcal per day during the first 6 months. After that add between 250 and 550 depending on how much of the baby's energy and nutrient needs are supplied by breastfeeding. As soon as weaning begins, the mother's energy needs begin to fall to pre-pregnancy levels.

Part 2
CARBOHYDRATES, FATS, & PROTEINS

In this part we discover essential nutritional facts about carbohydrates, proteins, and fats in food. Working through each in turn, we learn of their structure, their function within the body, and the relative proportions that we need of each for optimum health. We explore the differences between sugars and starches, plant and animal proteins, and the various types of fat, finding out which forms are the most beneficial to health. This is supplemented with dietary tips for meeting our daily requirements for fiber, essential amino acids, and essential fatty acids.

This information is followed by nutritional tables, which detail the calorie, protein, carbohydrate, and fat content of a range of foods, enabling you to create a more balanced diet.

All about carbohydrates

There are many types of carbohydrates, and most are essential sources of energy in the human diet. Most of the carbohydrate in food comes from plants, which convert sunlight into carbohydrate in a process called photosynthesis. The only significant animal sources of carbohydrate in the human diet are lactose from dairy products and fructose from honey.

Monosaccharides are carbohydrates that contain only one carbohydrate molecule. There are two different types of monosaccharide, glucose and fructose, both of which are found in fruits and vegetables. When two monosaccharides combine they form disaccharides, such as lactose, sucrose (table sugar), maltose (found in malted wheat and barley), and trehalose (found in mushrooms).

Polysaccharides are made up of chains of monosaccharides and come in two varieties: starch (complex carbohydrate) and non-starch polysaccharide (fiber). Plants store energy in the form of complex carbohydrate, which is found in large amounts in grains and roots. Fiber is found in plant cell walls where it plays a structural role.

CARBOHYDRATE DIGESTION

Glucose provides the fuel for all the body's metabolic activities. It is either absorbed directly from the digestive tract, or released from the breakdown of di- and polysaccharides into monosaccharides during digestion. Absorption is slowed by eating raw foods, starchy foods, and by the presence of protein and fats.

Carbohydrate digestion begins in the mouth where chewing breaks up the food and mixes it with a digestive enzyme called amylase. Gastric acid in the stomach breaks the food down further, but the main digestion occurs in the small intestine with the help of enzymes secreted by the pancreas.

Carbohydrate that escapes digestion in the small intestine is fermented in the large intestine, and turned into fatty acids and gas. The fatty acids are absorbed, and so is the gas to a certain extent, but if too much gas is produced it is expelled as wind. Absorbed gas is excreted through the lungs. The fermentation of small polysaccharides, such as inulin (found in dandelion root, Jerusalem artichoke, asparagus, onion, and garlic) stimulates the growth of bifidobacteria, and helps to protect the natural bacterial flora of the digestive tract.

CARBOHYDRATES AND HEALTH

Simple sugars (mono- and disaccharides) are found within the cell walls of fruits and vegetables, and can also be extracted from sugar cane, sugar beet, maple, corn, or honey. They are very easily absorbed into the bloodstream, and the quick energy boost they provide can seem very attractive when you are feeling low. However, an abundance of sugar in the blood is always followed by a corresponding release of insulin, which promotes the transportation of sugar into cells. This in turn causes a drop in blood-sugar levels, followed by a renewed feeling of lethargy and a craving for more sugar.

Refined sugar is a disaccharide made from sugar cane and sugar beets, leaving molasses as a by-product. It is associated with a range of health problems including tooth decay, obesity, diabetes, Crohn's disease, candida, heart disease, and cancer.

The average Westerner consumes between 65 and 70 lbs of refined sugar per year, mostly as an added ingredient in processed foods and drinks. "Raw" cane sugar is less refined and contains sucrose plus small quantities of micronutrients.

Complex carbohydrates (starch) are found in the cell walls of whole grains, vegetables, and raw fruits. During digestion, cell walls are broken down to make the carbohydrate accessible for absorption. Foods rich in complex carbohydrates are good for health for four reasons: they do not expose the teeth to the effects of "free" sugars; they slow the digestive process, producing a feeling of fullness; they help to maintain stable blood-sugar levels; and their non-digestible plant cell walls (fiber) provide bulk for the feces. Even though complex carbohydrates are made from the same building blocks as simple sugars, they release their sugar molecules at a much slower rate, producing a more measured insulin response and steadier blood-sugar and energy levels.

Fiber (non-starch polysaccharide) comes in two forms—soluble and insoluble. Soluble fiber (including pectins, gums, and mucilages) is easily digested whereas insoluble fiber (including cellulose, hemicellulose, and lignans) passes through the digestive tract undigested. A high intake of foods naturally rich in soluble and insoluble fiber reduces the risk of gallstones, and may also decrease the risk of coronary heart disease by lowering blood cholesterol levels. Insoluble fiber reduces the time it takes for food to pass through the gut by increasing the bulk of feces, and helps to protect against digestive disorders and cancer. Soluble fiber protects the lining of the digestive tract and reduces the risk of blood clot formation. Foods high in fiber also tend to be rich in health-protective micronutrients, such as vitamins, antioxidants, and phytochemicals, and help to improve the control of blood-sugar levels in diabetes. High-fiber diets give an average digestive "transit time" of 24 to 48 hours, compared with the average American diet, which gives an average transit time of 72 hours. A long intestinal transit time is a risk factor for diverticulitis and colon cancer.

Bran fiber (in wholewheat bread and some breakfast cereals) can, paradoxically, cause constipation because it absorbs water from the gut. If you eat a lot of bran, it is important to drink at least three pints of water a day to counter this effect. Eating an excess of foods with added fiber may also decrease the absorption of drugs, vitamins, minerals, and other nutrients.

ACRYLAMIDE

In April 2002, researchers at Stockholm University reported that they had found acrylamide in starchy foods fried at high temperatures. These findings attracted worldwide attention because acrylamide is thought to be associated with cancer, neurological damage, and infertility. Acrylamide is used in water purification, in the manufacture of cosmetics, plastics, and other industrial products, and as an additive to commercial herbicides. It is also found in tobacco smoke. At the moment it is not understood how acrylamide is formed in foods, but it may be the result of a natural chemical reaction caused by baking or frying foods for long periods at very high temperatures. The use of grains and vegetables that have been exposed to acrylamide-containing herbicides may also be implicated.

Food safety agencies are investigating the matter further, but do not advise people to change their diet on the basis of the current evidence. Whatever risk exists can be minimized by eating plenty of fresh organic foods, and by avoiding excessive high-temperature cooking and heat-treated processed foods.

All about proteins

Between ten and fifteen per cent of the calories we consume each day come from protein. Though it can be used as an energy source, the main purpose of protein is to provide the building blocks necessary for the growth and maintenance of body structures.

Proteins are complex chemicals, which come in many shapes and sizes. They all contain amino acids linked together into chains and folded into specific shapes. Protein chains vary in length from two to thousands of amino acids. There are twenty naturally occuring amino acids, and the proteins we eat contain varying amounts of each. The body is capable of converting most amino acids from one type to another according to need, but there are eight which it cannot make. These are the essential amino acids and must be obtained from the diet.

During digestion, protein is broken down into amino acids and then absorbed in the small intestine. After absorption, amino acids are transported to the liver for processing, and then distributed in the bloodstream to become part of enzymes, body cells, hormones, hair, nails, bones, muscles, and

DNA. The body is continually recombining amino acids to make new proteins, and nearly all body cells are capable of synthesizing specific proteins for their own purposes. Worn-out proteins are dismantled by the liver and excreted in the urine. The body maintains a protein reserve of between 10 and 14 oz to compensate for variations in protein intake.

As mentioned earlier, the absorption of carbohydrate into the bloodstream after a meal stimulates the release of insulin from the pancreas. In addition to promoting the uptake of glucose into the body's cells, insulin encourages protein synthesis in the muscles and liver, and inhibits protein breakdown. As long as there are calories available from carbohydrate, there is no need to use body protein for energy. Unlike fat and carbohydrate, protein is used as a source of energy only under exceptional circumstances, for example, in cases of starvation, serious injury, or major disease, such as cancer.

During fasting and in times of trauma or stress, another hormone called glucagon is released from the pancreas. Glucagon encourages the body to use amino acids instead of carbohydrates for fuel. The stress hormones, cortisol and adrenalin, act in a similar way, causing the protein in muscles to be broken down into free amino acids for conversion into energy. Trauma and stress can therefore cause the loss of substantial amounts of protein, especially from muscle tissue.

PROTEIN NEEDS

Nutritionists used to assume that, since protein is used to build and maintain body tissues, eating more protein must be good for us. It is now clear, however, that eating too much protein can lead to health problems, including osteoporosis and kidney disease. Human protein requirements change according to the need for growth, tissue repair, metabolism, and activity, but the current consensus is that a diet containing ten per cent protein is more than adequate to maintain health. Since nearly all foods contain at least ten per cent of their calories as protein, it follows that if you satisfy your calorie needs with good quality food, you will easily meet your protein requirements. In the developed world it is rare to see anyone protein deficient.

Earlier recommendations for human protein intake differentiated between "first class" animal proteins and "second class" plant proteins, on the basis that the animal proteins had an amino acid content similar to human body proteins. It has since been established that plant-based foods, such as grains, cereals, pulses, and vegetables, contain all the essential amino acids, albeit in different proportions. Far from being second class, plant proteins come packaged with other important nutrients, such as fiber and phytochemicals, and are also naturally low in fat and cholesterol.

Even the concept of essential amino acids is under review, since it is now understood that some essential amino acids can be made from other precursor chemicals in the diet, and some can be synthesized in the digestive tract. Essential amino acids are also recycled from worn-out proteins before these are excreted from the body. If no protein is eaten, 90 per cent of amino acids can be recycled.

All about fats

Fats are energy-dense foods containing more than twice as many calories, weight for weight, as carbohydrate or protein. They supply the body with essential fatty acids, carry fat-soluble vitamins, aid metabolism, and provide structure for cell membranes. They also make food taste good.

Fats contain fatty acids, which are long hydrocarbon chains with a "carboxyl group" attached to one end. There are three main types, classified according to the organization of the hydrogen atoms in their chains—saturated, monounsaturated, and polyunsaturated.

Saturated fatty acids have no room for additional hydrogen atoms on their hydrocarbon chains. This makes them very stable, and solid at room temperature. They are mainly found in meat, lard, butter, cheese, and milk.

Monounsaturated fatty acids have room for two extra hydrogen atoms and exist as thick oils at room temperature. Olive oil is mainly monounsaturated, and is thought to protect against heart disease by lowering blood cholesterol levels. It is the best choice for cooking because it reacts less to heat than saturated or polyunsaturated fats and oils.

Polyunsaturated fatty acids have room for more than two extra hydrogen atoms. They are sensitive to heat, light, and air, and tend to go rancid unless kept in a cool, dark place. Thin vegetable oils consist mostly of polyunsaturated fat and essential fatty acids (EFAs)—so called because they cannot be made by the body and therefore must be obtained from the diet.

Essential fatty acids keep blood vessels, nerves, skin, and other tissues in good condition and take part in the production of prostaglandins, which are important for normal immune function, cholesterol management, and blood clotting.

The two most important EFAs are linoleic acid (an omega-6 fatty acid) and linolenic acid, which exists in two forms, gamma-linolenic acid (an omega-6 fatty acid), and alpha-linolenic acid (an omega-3 fatty acid). Omega-6 fatty acids are found in most vegetable oils and are thought to lower blood cholesterol and Low Density Lipoproteins (see opposite). Oily fish, soy beans, evening primrose oil, walnuts, flax seeds, and pumpkin seeds are rich in omega-3 fatty acids, which reduce inflammation and protect the heart.

TRANS FATS

Saturated fats have a higher melting point than unsaturated fats, which makes them useful in food processing. Unsaturated fats are sometimes turned into saturated trans fats by a chemical process known as hydrogenation. Trans fats are linked to a number of health problems, including cancer, atherosclerosis, and infertility. To avoid trans fats, choose products marked "no trans fats" or "unhydrogenated" whenever possible.

BODY FAT

Body fat is our energy store, which we draw on whenever our diet is lacking in calories. Excess fat and carbohydrate in the diet increases the amount of body fat, while fasting causes fat breakdown. Many drugs and toxins find their way into fatty tissues, so fasting is a powerful way to detox the body.

CHOLESTEROL AND LIPOPROTEINS

Cholesterol and steroid hormones are made from sterols. High levels of cholesterol in the blood increase the risk of cardiovascular disease. Despite its bad reputation, cholesterol is a vital component of cell membranes, and is involved in the production of bile acids and sex hormones. It is not necessary to eat cholesterol, however, because the body makes all that it needs.

Meat, eggs, and dairy products tend to have a high cholesterol content. But it is not eating cholesterol per se that causes high blood cholesterol. The problem is that foods rich in cholesterol also tend to have a high saturated fat content. Excess saturated fat in the diet leads to high levels of Low Density Lipoproteins (LDLs) in the blood. Lipoproteins are fat molecules designed to transport fatty acids around the body. LDLs are the main carriers of cholesterol in the blood, and are known as "bad" lipoproteins because they are associated with high blood cholesterol levels. High Density Lipoproteins are known as "good" lipoproteins because they mop up excess cholesterol and return it to the liver for reprocessing and excretion. HDLs also remove cholesterol from clogged up arteries, helping to prevent cardiovascular disease.

FATS IN FOOD

Most foods contain at least some fat. Oily fish, vegetable oils, nuts, seeds, olives, avocados, meats, dairy products, butter, and table fats are all examples of high-fat foods, but the types of fatty acids they contain vary (see lists, opposite).

Olive oil is the best known source of monounsaturated fat. Vegetable foods contain mostly polyunsaturated fat and, together with oily fish, are the main sources of essential fatty acids in the diet.

In terms of their fat content, fish can be divided into two categories—lean and oily. Both contain monounsaturated and polyunsaturated fats. Virtually all of the fat in lean fish is found in the liver, whereas oily fish carry their fat reserves in the flesh. Oily fish and walnuts are good sources of omega-3 fatty acids.

Meat and dairy products (which contribute 23 per cent of the fat in the average Western diet) contain mostly saturated fats, and eggs contain a lot of cholesterol. However, the composition of the fat in meat and dairy products depends on the animals' diet and lifestyle. Active animals, fed on pasture and grains, have a lower saturated-fat content in their meat than those reared using intensive farming methods.

FATS IN FOODS

(Listed according to predominate fat type)

SATURATED	MONOUNSATURATED	POLYUNSATURATED
Beef	Almond oil	Brazil nuts
Burgers	Almonds	Cereals
Butter	Avocados	Corn oil
Cakes and cookies	Fish	Evening primrose oil
Cheese	Game★	Fish
Chocolate	Hazelnuts	Grouse
Cream	Low-fat spread	Pulses
Coconut	Olive oil	Safflower oil
Eggs	Olives	Sesame oil
Hydrogenated oil	Peanuts	Sesame seeds
Ice cream		Soft vegetable
Lamb		margarine
Lard		Soy beans
Margarine		Soy oil
Milk		Soy products
Palm oil		Sunflower oil
Pork		Sunflower seeds
Poultry		Vegetables
Sausages		Walnut oil
Suet		Walnuts
		Wheat germ oil

★Monounsaturated fats in meat and dairy products are sometimes present in the form of trans fats which have adverse effects on health.

FAT GUIDELINES

• Keep your daily fat intake at or below 30 per cent of your total calorie intake.

• Keep the ratio of unsaturated to saturated fat in your diet to at least 2:1 (that is to say, eat twice as many foods containing unsaturated fats as those containing saturated fats).

• Include omega-3 fatty acids in your diet by eating walnuts, flax seeds, and/or oily fish, or by taking drops of evening primrose or borage oil.

• Eat more low-fat protein foods, such as pulses, fish, and poultry, and reduce the amount of red meat, offal, eggs, and dairy products that you eat.

• Choose lean cuts of meat and trim off any excess fat.

• Limit the amount of fried foods you eat.

• If you eat dairy products, choose low-fat alternatives whenever possible.

• Keep foods that are rich in cholesterol (such as meat, dairy products, and eggs) to a minimum in your diet.

CARBOHYDRATE, FAT, AND PROTEIN TABLES

These tables provide a breakdown of the calorie, protein, carbohydrate, and fat content of a wide selection of foods. The calorie content of each food is given "per average portion" to allow you to work out the calorie content of your diet without the need for using weights and measures.

The carbohydrate, protein, and fat contents of each food are given as percentages of total calories. This enables you to compare the nutrient contents of foods with the Quality Calorie Targets (QCTs) for those nutrients, given at the top of the relevant columns. Total carbohydrate content is also broken down into simple sugars, complex carbohydrates, and fiber, and total fat is broken down to indicate the ratio of unsaturated to saturated fat, and the amount of cholesterol and essential fatty acids ("n" is given where the figure is not known, "tr" denotes trace). In addition, a quality-calorie points score indicates which foods have the best balance of nutrients.

FRUIT

FOOD	AVERAGE PORTION SIZE	TOTAL CALORIES	PROTEIN CONTENT	
(where appropriate, numbers in brackets represent number of fruit in average portion)	oz per portion	kcals per portion	% of kcals (QCT: 10% of total kcals)	grams per portion (QCT: men 55g/day; women 45g/day)
Fresh fruit				
Apple (1)	3 ½	47	3%	0.4
Apricot (2)	4 ½	40	12%	1.2
Date (4)	3 ½	124	5%	1.5
Fig (2)	4	47	12%	1.4
Grapes (bunch)	3 ½	60	3%	0.4
Kiwi fruit (2)	4	59	9%	1.3
Melon (all types) (1 slice)	6 ½	43	10%	1.1
Peach/nectarine (1)	5	55	13%	1.8
Pear (1)	6	68	3%	0.5
Persimmon (1)	4	80	4%	0.9
Plum/greengage (2)	3 ½	39	7%	0.7
Rhubarb	3 ½	7	51%	0.9
Tropical fruit				
Banana (1)	3 ½	95	5%	1.2
Guava (1)	5	36	12%	1.1
Lychee (5)	2 ½	44	6%	0.7
Mango (½)	6 ½	103	5%	1.3
Papaya/paw-paw (¼)	5	50	6%	0.7
Passionfruit (5)	2 ½	27	29%	2.0
Pineapple (2 slices)	5 ½	66	4%	0.6
Pomegranate (1)	3 ½	51	10%	1.3
Citrus fruit				
Clementine/satsuma/tangerine (2)	4	43	10%	1.1
Grapefruit/pomelo (1)	6 ½	54	11%	1.4
Lemon/lime (1)	3 ½	12	23%	0.8
Orange (1)	5 ½	59	12%	1.8
Berries				
Blackberries (20)	3 ½	25	14%	0.9
Blackcurrants	3 ½	28	13%	0.9

continues

	CARBOHYDRATE CONTENT					FAT CONTENT			QUALITY CALORIE POINTS
% of kcals (QCI: 60% of total kcals)	% of carbs as simple carbs	% of carbs as complex carbs	fiber in grams per portion (QCT: 16–24g/day)	% of kcals (QCT: less than 30% of total kcals)	unsat./sat. fat ratio (QCI: at least 2:1)*	cholesterol in mg per portion	EFAs in grams per portion (QCT: at least 5g/day)	max 100
95%	100%	0%	2.0	2%	n	0	n	75
85%	99%	1%	2.5	3%	n	0	n	75
94%	100%	0%	3.6	1%	n	0	n	73
82%	100%	0%	2.5	6%	n	0	n	75
96%	100%	0%	0.8	1%	n	0	n	71
82%	97%	3%	2.3	9%	n	0	n	77
86%	100%	0%	1.6	4%	n	0	n	76
85%	100%	0%	3.4	2%	n	0	n	76
95%	100%	0%	3.7	2%	n	0	n	74
95%	100%	0%	1.8	1%	n	0	n	81
91%	100%	0%	2.3	2%	n	0	n	74
43%	100%	0%	2.3	6%	n	0	n	76
92%	90%	10%	3.1	3%	n	0	n	76
71%	98%	2%	6.6	17%	n	0	n	81
92%	100%	0%	1.1	2%	n	0	n	75
92%	98%	2%	5.2	3%	n	0	n	80
91%	100%	0%	3.2	3%	n	0	n	77
61%	100%	0%	2.5	10%	n	0	n	81
92%	100%	0%	2.1	4%	n	0	n	75
86%	100%	0%	3.4	4%	n	0	n	77
87%	100%	0%	2.0	3%	n	0	n	76
86%	100%	0%	2.9	3%	n	0	n	76
58%	100%	0%	1.6	19%	n	0	n	80
86%	100%	0%	2.9	2%	n	0	n	76
79%	100%	0%	6.6	7%	n	0	n	81
86%	100%	0%	7.8	1%	n	0	n	82

*0.5 means half as much unsaturated fat as saturated fat; 2.0 means twice as much

FRUIT

FOOD	AVERAGE PORTION SIZE	TOTAL CALORIES	PROTEIN CONTENT	
(where appropriate, numbers in brackets represent number of fruit in average portion)	oz per portion	kcals per portion	% of kcals (QCT: 10% of total kcals)	grams per portion (QCT: men 55g/day; women 45g/day)
Blueberries (bilberries)	3 ½	30	8%	0.6
Cherries (10)	3 ½	48	8%	0.9
Cranberries	3 ½	15	11%	0.4
Elderberries	3 ½	35	8%	0.7
Gooseberries	3 ½	40	6%	0.7
Raspberries (25)	3 ½	25	22%	1.4
Redcurrants	3 ½	21	21%	1.1
Strawberries (10)	4	32	12%	1.0
Dried fruit				
Apricot (10)	3 ½	132	10%	3.4
Date (6)	3 ½	203	5%	2.5
Fig (5)	3 ½	227	6%	2.2
Pear (10 slices)	3 ½	207	3%	0.8
Pineapple (6 slices)	3 ½	276	4%	1.3
Prune (10)	3 ½	160	7%	1.4
Raisins (3 tbs)	3 ½	163	3%	1.3

CARBOHYDRATE CONTENT					FAT CONTENT				QUALITY CALORIE POINTS
% of kcals (QCI: 60% of total kcals)	% of carbs as simple carbs	% of carbs as complex carbs	fiber in grams per portion (QCI: 16–24g/day)	% of kcals (QCI: less than 30% of total kcals)	unsat./sat. fat ratio (QCI: at least 2:1)*	cholesterol in mg per portion	EFAs in grams per portion (QCI: at least 5g/day)		max 100
86%	100%	0%	2.5	6%	n	0	n		87
90%	100%	0%	0.2	2%	n	0	n		75
83%	100%	0%	3.8	6%	n	0	n		80
79%	100%	0%	n	13%	n	0	n		80
84%	100%	0%	3.1	10%	n	0	n		77
67%	100%	0%	6.7	11%	n	0	n		83
78%	100%	0%	7.4	1%	n	0	n		82
85%	100%	0%	2.4	3%	n	0	n		79
87%	100%	0%	15.1	3%	n	0	n		88
94%	100%	0%	5.9	1%	n	0	n		76
88%	100%	0%	7.4	6%	n	0	n		79
95%	100%	0%	10.8	2%	n	0	n		74
92%	100%	0%	4.4	4%	n	0	n		75
90%	100%	0%	7.3	3%	n	0	n		78
96%	100%	0%	3.7	1%	n	0	n		71

*0.5 means half as much unsaturated fat as saturated fat; 2.0 means twice as much

NUTS AND SEEDS

FOOD	AVERAGE PORTION SIZE	TOTAL CALORIES	PROTEIN CONTENT	
	oz per portion	kcals per portion	% of kcals (QCT: 10% of total kcals)	grams per portion (QCT: men 55g/day; women 45g/day)
Almonds	1 3/4	306	14%	10.6
Brazil nuts	1 3/4	341	8%	7.1
Cashew nuts	1 3/4	287	12%	8.9
Chestnuts, dried	1 3/4	160	5%	1.9
Coconut, fresh	3 1/2	351	4%	3.2
Coconut, desiccated	1 3/4	302	4%	2.8
Hazelnuts	1 3/4	325	9%	7.1
Macadamia nuts (salted)	1 3/4	374	4%	4.0
Melon seeds	1 3/4	292	20%	14.3
Peanuts	1 3/4	282	18%	12.8
Peanut butter	3/4	125	15%	4.5
Pecan nuts	1 3/4	345	5%	4.6
Pine nuts	1 3/4	344	8%	7.0
Pistachio nuts (salted)	1 3/4	301	12%	9.0
Pumpkin seeds	1 3/4	285	17%	12.2
Sesame seeds	1 3/4	299	12%	9.1
Sesame spread (tahini)	1 3/4	304	12%	9.3
Sunflower seeds	1 3/4	291	14%	9.9
Walnuts	1 3/4	344	9%	7.4

CARBOHYDRATE CONTENT					FAT CONTENT				QUALITY CALORIE POINTS
% of kcals (QCT: 60% of total kcals)	% of carbs as simple carbs	% of carbs as complex carbs	fiber in grams per portion (QCT: 16–24g/day)	% of kcals (QCT: less than 30% of total kcals)	unsat./sat. fat ratio (QCT: at least 2:1)*	cholesterol in mg per portion	EFAs in grams per portion (QCT: at least 5g/day)		max 100
4%	61%	39%	6.5	82%	10.3	0	7.1		71
2%	77%	23%	4.1	90%	3.0	0	11.5		64
12%	25%	75%	1.6	76%	3.9	0	4.4		67
81%	19%	81%	5.8	14%	4.4	0	1.1		77
4%	100%	0%	12.2	92%	0.1	0	0.8		47
4%	100%	0%	10.6	92%	0.1	0	0.8		48
3%	67%	33%	4.5	88%	11.9	0	3.0		63
3%	83%	17%	2.7	93%	5.6	0	0.8		45
6%	n	n	n	74%	2.9	0	13.1		69
8%	50%	50%	3.7	74%	4.3	0	7.2		68
7%	51%	49%	1.4	78%	3.4	0	3.7		59
3%	74%	26%	2.4	92%	10.7	0	9.4		66
2%	97%	3%	1.0	90%	13.3	0	20.6		74
5%	69%	31%	3.1	83%	6.1	0	9.0		68
10%	7%	93%	2.7	73%	4.2	0	9.2		67
1%	44%	56%	4.0	87%	5.7	0	12.8		67
1%	44%	56%	4.0	87%	5.7	0	12.9		69
12%	9%	91%	3.0	74%	9.1	0	15.5		79
2%	79%	21%	3.0	89%	10.7	0	23.8		81

*0.5 means half as much unsaturated fat as saturated fat; 2.0 means twice as much

VEGETABLES AND PULSES

FOOD	AVERAGE PORTION SIZE	TOTAL CALORIES	PROTEIN CONTENT	
	oz per portion	kcals per portion	% of kcals (QCT: 10% of total kcals)	grams per portion (QCT: men 55g/day; women 45g/day)
Root vegetables				
Beet	3 1/2	36	19%	1.7
Carrot	3 1/2	35	7%	0.6
Celeriac	3 1/2	18	29%	1.2
Parsnip	3 1/2	64	11%	1.8
Potato, baked	6 1/2	245	11%	7.0
Potato, boiled in salted water	6 1/2	130	10%	3.2
Potato, mashed	6 1/2	187	7%	3.2
Potato, fries (all types, average)	6 1/2	398	6%	6.1
Rutabaga	3 1/2	24	12%	0.7
Sweet potato, baked	4 1/2	150	6%	2.1
Beans, peas, and lentils				
Aduki beans, cooked	3 1/2	123	30%	9.3
Baked beans, in tomato sauce	4 1/2	105	24%	6.2
Bean sprouts, fresh	2	19	37%	1.7
Blackeye/pigeon/mung beans (av.)	3 1/2	99	33%	8.1
Chick peas, cooked	3 1/2	121	28%	8.4
Fava beans, fresh	4	71	39%	6.8
Green beans (haricots verts), fresh	3 1/2	24	32%	1.9
Haricot beans, dried, cooked	3 1/2	95	28%	6.6
Lentils, cooked (all types, average)	3 1/2	105	34%	8.8
Lima beans, cooked	3 1/2	103	28%	7.1
Peas, fresh	3 1/2	83	33%	6.9
Pinto beans, cooked	3 1/2	137	27%	8.9
Red kidney beans, cooked	3 1/2	103	33%	8.4
String beans, yard-long, fresh	3 1/2	22	29%	1.6
Soy beans, black, cooked	3 1/2	141	40%	14.0
Tempeh (fermented soybean)	3 1/2	166	50%	20.7
Tofu (soybean curd)	3 1/2	73	44%	8.1

continues

	CARBOHYDRATE CONTENT					FAT CONTENT			QUALITY CALORIE POINTS
% of kcals (QCT: 60% of total kcals)	% of carbs as simple carbs	% of carbs as complex carbs	fiber in grams per portion (QCT: 16–24g/day)	% of kcals (QCT: less than 30% of total kcals)	unsat./sat. fat ratio (QCT: at least 2:1)*	cholesterol in mg per portion	EFAs in grams per portion (QCT: at least 5g/day)	max 100
78%	97%	3%	2.8	3%	n	0	n	**80**
85%	96%	4%	2.6	8%	n	0	n	**75**
50%	78%	22%	5.1	21%	n	0	n	**80**
74%	48%	52%	4.3	15%	n	0	n	**81**
88%	4%	96%	4.9	1%	6.0	0	0.1	**79**
89%	4%	96%	2.5	1%	6.0	0	0.1	**76**
56%	6%	94%	2.3	37%	n	0	n	**74**
54%	2%	98%	5.4	40%	n	0	n	**61**
77%	98%	2%	2.4	11%	6.7	0	0.2	**80**
91%	52%	48%	3.9	3%	1.0	0	0.3	**72**
69%	2%	98%	11.1	1%	n	0	n	**85**
69%	38%	62%	8.6	7%	3.8	0	0.4	**79**
48%	55%	45%	3.4	15%	n	0	n	**82**
62%	1%	99%	5.3	5%	n	0	n	**86**
56%	6%	94%	5.1	16%	n	0	n	**83**
46%	19%	81%	7.3	15%	n	0	n	**87**
49%	72%	28%	3.0	19%	n	0	n	**82**
67%	6%	94%	22.9	5%	n	0	n	**91**
60%	2%	98%	3.8	6%	n	0	n	**83**
67%	9%	91%	4.6	5%	n	0	n	**81**
51%	25%	75%	4.7	16%	1.0	0	tr	**73**
67%	n	n	n	6%	n	0	n	**85**
63%	6%	94%	9.0	4%	n	0	n	**89**
55%	88%	12%	2.6	16%	11.0	0	0.1	**84**
13%	52%	48%	6.1	47%	n	0	n	**76**
15%	16%	84%	4.1	35%	n	0	n	**78**
4%	50%	50%	0.3	52%	n	0	n	**77**

*0.5 means half as much unsaturated fat as saturated fat; 2.0 means twice as much

VEGETABLES AND PULSES

FOOD	AVERAGE PORTION SIZE	TOTAL CALORIES	PROTEIN CONTENT	
(where appropriate, numbers in brackets represent number of vegetables in average portion)	oz per portion	kcals per portion	% of kcals (QCT: 10% of total kcals)	grams per portion (QCT: men 55g/day; women 45g/day)
Miscellaneous vegetables				
Artichoke hearts (2)	3 ½	18	62%	2.8
Asparagus (5 spears)	4 ½	31	46%	3.6
Avocado (1)	5	276	4%	2.8
Beet greens	3 ½	33	36%	3.0
Broccoli, green/purple	3 ½	34	49%	4.2
Brussels sprouts (9)	3 ½	42	33%	3.5
Cabbage (all types, average)	3 ½	26	26%	1.7
Cauliflower	3 ½	34	42%	3.6
Celery (3 sticks)	3 ½	7	29%	0.5
Chicory	3 ½	13	55%	1.8
Cucumber (2 in chunk)	4	12	28%	0.4
Curly kale	3 ½	33	41%	3.4
Eggplant (½)	4 ½	20	24%	1.2
Fennel	3 ½	12	30%	0.9
Lettuce (all types, average)	2 ¾	10	30%	0.7
Mushrooms, common	3 ½	13	55%	1.8
Mushrooms, shiitake	1 ¾	28	12%	0.8
Okra (gumbo)	3 ½	31	36%	2.8
Olive (10)	1	31	3%	0.3
Onion/leek (all types, average)	3 ½	28	19%	1.3
Pepper, green/red (½)	2 ¾	19	15%	0.7
Pumpkin	6 ½	23	22%	1.3
Seaweed, dried (all types, average)	½	8	80%	1.7
Spinach	3 ½	25	45%	2.8
Sweetcorn	3 ½	93	15%	3.4
Swiss chard	3 ½	19	38%	1.8
Tomato (1)	3	14	16%	0.6
Watercress	3	18	54%	2.4
Zucchini	3 ½	18	40%	0.9

	CARBOHYDRATE CONTENT				FAT CONTENT			QUALITY CALORIE POINTS
% of kcals (QCI: 60% of total kcals)	% of carbs as simple carbs	% of carbs as complex carbs	fiber in grams per portion (QCI: 16–24g/day)	% of kcals (QCI: less than 30% of total kcals)	unsat./sat. fat ratio (QCI: at least 2:1)*	cholesterol in mg per portion	EFAs in grams per portion (QCI: at least 5g/day)	max 100
28%	98%	2%	n	10%	n	0	n	78
30%	95%	5%	2.1	24%	n	0	n	79
4%	98%	2%	4.9	92%	7.1	0	2.8	65
35%	87%	13%	6.1	28%	5.5	0	0.3	78
24%	92%	8%	4.2	27%	n	0	n	72
37%	79%	21%	3.8	30%	n	0	n	79
59%	98%	2%	2.9	15%	n	0	n	85
33%	86%	14%	1.9	25%	n	0	n	74
48%	99%	1%	1.6	23%	n	0	n	82
29%	99%	1%	2.0	16%	n	0	n	73
52%	93%	7%	0.8	20%	n	0	n	78
16%	93%	7%	3.3	43%	5.5	0	0.3	72
55%	91%	9%	3.0	21%	n	0	n	85
56%	94%	6%	2.4	14%	n	0	n	75
37%	99%	1%	1.0	33%	n	0	n	74
12%	50%	50%	2.3	33%	2.5	0	0.3	64
83%	n	n	n	5%	n	0	n	80
36%	83%	17%	4.5	28%	n	0	n	78
1%	tr	0%	1.2	96%	5.8	0	0.4	53
76%	96%	4%	2.2	5%	n	0	n	80
70%	98%	2%	1.5	15%	4.0	0	0.2	82
63%	85%	15%	0.9	15%	n	0	n	84
tr	-	-	5.0	20%	n	0	n	65
24%	94%	6%	3.9	31%	5.5	0	0.3	75
68%	12%	88%	3.3	17%	4.9	0	1.9	83
57%	21%	79%	n	5%	5.5	0	0.3	85
69%	99%	1%	1.1	15%	n	0	n	82
7%	98%	2%	2.4	39%	n	0	n	65
38%	94%	6%	0.9	23%	1.3	0	tr	68

*0.5 means half as much unsaturated fat as saturated fat; 2.0 means twice as much

VEGETABLE DISHES

FOOD	AVERAGE PORTION SIZE	TOTAL CALORIES	PROTEIN CONTENT	
(where appropriate, numbers in brackets represent number of items in average portion)	oz per portion	kcals per portion	% of kcals (QCT: 10% of total kcals)	grams per portion (QCT: men 55g/day; women 45g/day)
Bakes and flans				
Cannelloni	7	**290**	12%	8.7
Casserole, bean and vegetable	9	**115**	24%	7.0
Cauliflower cheese	7	**210**	23%	12.1
Cottage pie, vegetable	10	**339**	16%	13.8
Flan, vegetable	4	**253**	10%	6.4
Lasagne, vegetable	16	**527**	16%	21.6
Moussaka, vegetable	12	**480**	13%	16.1
Nut roast	5	**528**	15%	20.0
Pizza, cheese and tomato	10	**711**	15%	27.3
Burgers, cutlets, and pancakes				
Beanburger (no bun)	2 ½	**152**	12%	4.7
Dosa with vegetable filling (1)	7	**307**	15%	11.6
Falafel (3)	3 ½	**179**	14%	6.4
Nut cutlet (2)	4	**347**	7%	5.8
Onion bhaji/pakora (1)	1 ¾	**156**	6%	2.3
Pancake with vegetable filling (1)	7	**298**	11%	8.2
Quorn (myco-protein)	3 ½	**86**	55%	11.8
Samosa, vegetable (1)	3 ½	**217**	9%	5.1
Tempeh burger (1)	2	**116**	16%	4.6
Tofu burger (1)	2	**71**	28%	4.9
Vegeburger (1)	2	**147**	26%	9.5
Curries, stews, and rice dishes				
Bhaji, cauliflower	9	**535**	7%	10.0
Bhaji, mushroom	9	**415**	4%	4.3
Bhaji, potato	9	**395**	6%	5.8
Broccoli in cheese sauce	7	**236**	22%	13.0
Colcannon (fried)	7	**248**	5%	2.8
Curry, cauliflower and potato	9	**148**	23%	8.5
Curry, chick pea and spinach	9	**498**	12%	15.0

continues

	CARBOHYDRATE CONTENT					FAT CONTENT		QUALITY CALORIE POINTS
% of kcals (QCT: 60% of total kcals)	% of carbs as simple carbs	% of carbs as complex carbs	fiber in grams per portion (QCT: 16–24g/day)	% of kcals (QCT: less than 30% of total kcals)	unsat./sat. fat ratio (QCT: at least 2:1)*	cholesterol in mg per portion	EFAs in grams per portion (QCT: at least 5g/day)	max 100
33%	19%	81%	2.0	55%	1.5	30	4.6	**70**
63%	49%	51%	5.5	13%	4.0	0	0.8	**86**
19%	58%	42%	2.8	58%	0.9	26	2.6	**61**
52%	9%	91%	7.8	32%	8.0	0	5.7	**92**
36%	13%	87%	2.0	54%	1.8	12	4.8	**75**
43%	33%	67%	7.2	41%	1.0	27	2.3	**70**
25%	29%	71%	5.6	62%	2.1	91	9.8	**77**
19%	17%	83%	8.1	66%	5.2	0	11.3	**83**
40%	9%	91%	5.7	45%	1.1	66	6.3	**75**
40%	20%	80%	4.6	48%	7.3	0	3.8	**75**
42%	14%	86%	6.0	43%	8.0	0	6.8	**78**
33%	17%	83%	4.4	53%	8.4	0	5.3	**68**
24%	7%	93%	3.2	69%	7.4	0	12.6	**68**
27%	15%	85%	3.5	67%	7.9	0	3.6	**67**
39%	26%	74%	2.4	50%	1.9	60	5.0	**68**
9%	55%	45%	4.8	36%	n	n	n	**78**
52%	9%	91%	n	39%	n	0	n	**76**
46%	5%	95%	1.3	38%	5.8	0	1.7	**64**
42%	21%	79%	1.3	30%	4.8	0	1.1	**62**
11%	45%	55%	2.2	63%	n	n	n	**49**
7%	80%	20%	5.5	86%	7.7	0	9.9	**76**
10%	68%	32%	5.0	86%	7.9	0	7.8	**75**
39%	9%	91%	4.0	55%	8.2	0	4.7	**85**
15%	54%	46%	3.0	63%	0.8	42	2.0	**56**
29%	14%	86%	3.8	66%	7.5	0	8.6	**70**
42%	39%	61%	4.8	35%	5.7	0	2.8	**82**
24%	7%	93%	10.8	64%	7.8	0	17.3	**91**

*0.5 means half as much unsaturated fat as saturated fat; 2.0 means twice as much

VEGETABLE DISHES

FOOD	AVERAGE PORTION SIZE	TOTAL CALORIES	PROTEIN CONTENT	
(where appropriate, numbers in brackets represent number of items in average portion)	oz per portion	kcals per portion	% of kcals (QCT: 10% of total kcals)	grams per portion (QCT: men 55g/day; women 45g/day)
Curry, red lentil and mung bean	9	285	17%	12.0
Curry, red lentil and tomato	9	230	14%	8.0
Curry, okra	9	273	10%	6.5
Curry, mixed vegetable	9	123	11%	3.5
Okra with tomato and onion	9	450	6%	7.3
Ratatouille	9	205	6%	3.3
Risotto (brown rice)	12	501	11%	14.4
Side dishes, dips, spreads, and sauces				
Guacamole	3 ½	128	4%	1.4
Houmous	2	112	16%	4.6
Pesto sauce	1	129	16%	5.1
Red cabbage, stewed with apple	3 ½	59	6%	0.9
Tofu spread	1 ¾	104	9%	2.3
Vegetable pâté	1 ¾	87	17%	3.8
Vegetable stir-fry	3 ½	64	13%	2.0
Vine leaves, stuffed with rice (3)	3 ½	262	4%	2.8
Salads				
Coleslaw, with vinaigrette	3 ½	87	5%	1.1
Salad, bean, with vinaigrette	3 ½	147	11%	4.2
Salad, beet, with vinaigrette	3 ½	100	8%	2.0
Salad, carrot, nut, with vinaigrette	3 ½	218	4%	2.1
Salad, Greek	3 ½	130	8%	2.7
Salad, green (no dressing)	3 ½	12	23%	0.7
Salad, pasta, veg., with mayonnaise	3 ½	127	8%	2.6
Salad, potato, with vinaigrette	3 ½	157	4%	1.5
Salad, potato, with mayonnaise	3 ½	239	3%	1.6
Salad, Waldorf	3 ½	193	3%	1.4
Tabouleh/couscous salad	3 ½	119	9%	2.6

CARBOHYDRATE CONTENT					FAT CONTENT				QUALITY CALORIE POINTS
% of kcals (QCT: 60% of total kcals)	% of carbs as simple carbs	% of carbs as complex carbs	fiber in grams per portion (QCT: 16–24g/day)	% of kcals (QCT: less than 30% of total kcals)	unsat./sat. fat ratio (QCT: at least 2:1)*	cholesterol in mg per portion	EFAs in grams per portion (QCT: at least 5g/day)		max 100
32%	9%	91%	5.5	51%	7.9	0	8.0		**86**
34%	29%	71%	4.8	52%	7.5	0	6.5		**88**
18%	77%	23%	9.0	72%	7.0	0	10.3		**83**
52%	52%	48%	4.0	37%	2.2	0	2.0		**79**
11%	82%	18%	11.5	83%	5.3	0	5.3		**80**
18%	84%	16%	5.0	76%	7.3	0	8.5		**81**
49%	14%	86%	12.6	40%	5.7	0	8.8		**98**
7%	59%	41%	2.6	89%	3.5	0	1.5		**56**
23%	17%	83%	1.9	61%	n	0	n		**73**
1%	75%	25%	n	83%	2.5	11	2.5		**51**
51%	94%	6%	2.7	43%	2.9	0	1.2		**76**
4%	67%	33%	0.3	87%	5.5	0	5.8		**64**
13%	3%	97%	n	70%	n	tr	n		**64**
38%	61%	39%	n	50%	6.0	0	2.1		**76**
34%	44%	56%	2.9	62%	5.6	0	2.2		**66**
54%	98%	2%	1.9	41%	6.4	0	2.3		**80**
33%	20%	80%	3.7	56%	7.6	0	4.2		**78**
31%	90%	10%	2.0	61%	8.1	0	3.2		**75**
23%	96%	4%	3.2	·73%	8.8	0	5.8		**78**
6%	100%	tr	1.1	86%	2.6	9	1.3		**54**
57%	94%	6%	1.2	20%	10.0	0	0.1		**84**
39%	17%	83%	2.1	53%	5.4	6	4.3		**71**
33%	7%	93%	1.3	63%	7.8	0	5.1		**80**
19%	9%	91%	1.1	78%	5.6	20	12.0		**71**
14%	99%	1%	1.7	83%	6.3	13	10.7		**71**
54%	4%	96%	n	37%	8.8	0	2.0		**86**

*0.5 means half as much unsaturated fat as saturated fat; 2.0 means twice as much

MEAT AND MEAT DISHES

FOOD	AVERAGE PORTION SIZE	TOTAL CALORIES	PROTEIN CONTENT	
	oz per portion	kcals per portion	% of kcals (QCT: 10% of total kcals)	grams per portion (QCT: men 55g/day; women 45g/day)
Beef				
Ground	7	458	40%	46.2
Roast	4	341	33%	28.1
Steak	4	295	47%	17.5
Veal cutlet	5	323	58%	47.1
Lamb				
Chop	5 ½	443	27%	29.3
Cutlet	3 ½	244	25%	15.2
Roast	4	319	39%	31.3
Pork				
Bacon	3 ½	477	20%	24.1
Chop	4	395	19%	19.1
Roast	4	343	38%	32.3
Poultry and game				
Chicken, roast	4	259	42%	27.1
Duck, roast	4	407	23%	23.5
Goose, roast	4	383	37%	35.2
Grouse, roast	4	208	72%	37.6
Pheasant, roast	4	256	61%	38.6
Rabbit, roast or stewed	4	230	62%	35.9
Squab, roast	4	276	48%	33.4
Turkey, roast	4	205	66%	33.6
Venison, roast or stewed	4	238	71%	42.0
Variety meats				
Heart (all types, average)	3 ½	208	55%	18.0
Kidney (all types, average)	3 ½	160	62%	24.9
Liver (all types, average)	3 ½	213	44%	24.2
Oxtail	3 ½	243	50%	30.5
Tripe	5	150	59%	22.2

continues

	CARBOHYDRATE CONTENT				FAT CONTENT			QUALITY CALORIE POINTS
% of kcals (QCI: 60% of total kcals)	% of carbs as simple carbs	% of carbs as complex carbs	fiber in grams per portion (QCT: 16–24g/day)	% of kcals (QCI: less than 30% of total kcals)	unsat./sat. fat ratio (QCI: at least 2:1)*	cholesterol in mg per portion	EFAs in grams per portion (QCT: at least 5g/day)	max 100
0%	-	-	0	60%	1.2	164	1.2	53
0%	-	-	0	67%	1.2	98	1.0	44
0%	-	-	0	53%	1.2	98	0.7	48
8%	n	n	n	34%	1.2	89	0.5	52
0%	-	-	0	73%	0.9	176	1.7	44
0%	-	-	0	75%	0.9	110	1.0	42
0%	-	-	0	61%	0.9	132	1.0	44
	-	-						
0%	-	-	0	80%	1.3	80	3.1	46
0%	-	-	0	81%	1.3	132	2.2	47
0%	-	-	0	62%	1.6	132	1.8	49
0%	-	-	0	58%	1.8	120	2.5	52
0%	-	-	0	77%	2.4	192	4.2	55
0%	-	-	0	63%	n	n	n	53
0%	-	-	0	28%	3.0	n	3.7	61
0%	-	-	0	39%	1.8	n	1.4	54
0%	-	-	0	38%	1.3	85	3	63
0%	-	-	0	52%	n	n	n	54
0%	-	-	0	34%	1.7	96	2.5	57
0%	-	-	0	29%	n	n	n	57
0%	-	-	0	45%	0.9	240	0.8	45
0%	-	-	0	38%	0.9	670	0.7	40
0%	-	-	0	46%	1.3	322	1.6	55
0%	-	-	0	50%	1.2	110	0.5	46
0%	-	-	0	41%	0.7	240	0.1	40

*0.5 means half as much unsaturated fat as saturated fat; 2.0 means twice as much

MEAT AND MEAT DISHES

FOOD	AVERAGE PORTION SIZE	TOTAL CALORIES	PROTEIN CONTENT	
(where appropriate, numbers in brackets represent number of items in average portion)	oz per portion	kcals per portion	% of kcals (QCT: 10% of total kcals)	grams per portion (QCT: men 55g/day; women 45g/day)
Cold meats				
Corned beef	1	54	50%	6.7
Ham	1	30	62%	4.6
Processed meat	1	78	16%	3.2
Tongue (pressed)	1	53	30%	4.0
Burgers and sausages				
Beefburger, quarterpounder	2 ³/₄	211	31%	16.3
Liver sausage (1)	1 ³/₄	155	17%	6.5
Salami (2 slices)	1	167	16%	6.6
Sausage (all types, average) (1)	1 ³/₄	157	13%	5.0
Turkey burger/escalope	3 ¼	119	90%	26.8
Meat dishes				
Black pudding	2 ½	229	17%	9.7
Bolognese sauce	7 ³/₄	306	23%	17.6
Chicken chow mein	12	515	24%	29.8
Cornish pasty	5 ½	515	10%	12.4
Cottage pie	10	357	26%	22.8
Haggis	3 ½	310	14%	10.7
Hot pot	11 ½	376	33%	30.7
Irish stew	11 ½	409	17%	17.2
Lamb curry	11 ½	528	23%	31.7
Lasagne	12	669	20%	34.3
Moussaka	11 ½	644	19%	30.7
Pork pie	5	564	10%	14.7
Samosa (lamb)	3 ½	578	5%	6.4
Sausage roll	2	287	6%	4.3
Shish kebab (in pita with salad)	9 ½	419	34%	36.5
Spring roll	3 ½	242	11%	6.5
Steak and kidney pie	7	646	12%	18.6
Tandoori chicken	12	749	51%	95.9

	CARBOHYDRATE CONTENT					FAT CONTENT			QUALITY CALORIE POINTS
% of kcals (QCI: 60% of total kcals)	% of carbs as simple carbs	% of carbs as complex carbs	fiber in grams per portion (QCI: 16–24g/day)	% of kcals (QCI: less than 30% of total kcals)	unsat./sat. fat ratio (QCI: at least 2:1)*	cholesterol in mg per portion	EFAs in grams per portion (QCI: at least 5g/day)	max 100
0%	-	-	0	50%	1.2	21	0.1	**44**
0%	-	-	0	38%	1.5	8	0.1	**47**
7%	n	n	n	77%	1.5	13	0.6	**46**
0%	-	-	0	70%	1.4	38	0.3	**44**
10%	n	n	n	59%	1.2	54	0.6	**46**
5%	n	n	n	78%	1.5	60	1.0	**47**
1%	n	n	n	83%	1.3	27	1.2	**39**
10%	n	n	n	77%	1.1	25	0.9	**45**
0%	-	-	0	10%	1.7	56	0.4	**54**
18%	n	n	n	65%	n	51	n	**56**
7%	n	n	n	70%	2.0	55	5.7	**66**
32%	4%	96%	3.9	44%	4.8	46	6.3	**78**
35%	n	n	n	55%	n	76	n	**69**
28%	n	n	n	46%	1.3	75	1.2	**59**
23%	n	n	n	63%	n	91	n	**62**
34%	n	n	n	33%	1.2	83	0.6	**58**
30%	n	n	n	53%	1.0	116	1.1	**57**
18%	n	n	n	59%	2.0	83	10	**70**
29%	19%	81%	2.8	51%	1.2	91	4.9	**70**
19%	n	n	n	62%	1.7	132	10.3	**72**
25%	n	n	n	65%	n	78	n	**61**
12%	n	n	n	83%	n	30	n	**44**
26%	n	n	n	68%	1.4	12	2.4	**44**
42%	11%	89%	2.7	24%	1.4	89	1.4	**65**
28%	13%	87%	1.9	61%	3.1	7	4.8	**62**
11%	n	n	n	37%	1.2	250	4.4	**64**
4%	50%	50%	tr	45%	2.1	420	7.0	**63**

*0.5 means half as much unsaturated fat as saturated fat; 2.0 means twice as much

FISH AND FISH DISHES

FOOD	AVERAGE PORTION SIZE	TOTAL CALORIES	PROTEIN CONTENT	
	oz per portion	kcals per portion	% of kcals (QCI: 10% of total kcals)	grams per portion (QCI: men 55g/day; women 45g/day)
White fish				
Cod, fried in batter	4	239	39%	23.5
Cod, grilled	4	114	88%	25.0
Haddock, fried	4	209	49%	25.7
Plaice, fried in batter	4	308	24%	18.3
Skate, fried in batter	4	202	35%	17.6
Sole, flounder, steamed	4	109	91%	24.7
Oily fish				
Anchovies, canned	½	29	53%	3.8
Herring, grilled	4	217	44%	24.1
Kipper, grilled	4	306	32%	24.1
Mackerel, smoked	5	531	21%	28.4
Salmon, canned	1 ¾	77	61%	11.8
Salmon, grilled	3 ½	215	45%	24.2
Salmon, smoked	1 ¾	71	72%	12.7
Sardines, canned	3 ½	172	50%	21.5
Sardines, in tomato sauce	1 ¾	72	46%	8.4
Trout, grilled	4	162	64%	25.8
Tuna, canned	3 ½	99	95%	23.5
Seafood				
Lobster, boiled	3 ¼	93	86%	19.9
Mussels, boiled	1 ½	42	64%	6.7
Prawns/shrimp, boiled	2	59	91%	13.6
Squid (calamare), fried in batter	2 ¼	127	24%	7.5
Fish products and dishes				
Cod roe, fried	4	242	41%	25.1
Fish sticks	2	143	24%	8.5
Pasta with seafood	9	275	32%	22.3
Taramasalata	1 ¾	252	3%	1.6

	CARBOHYDRATE CONTENT				FAT CONTENT			QUALITY CALORIE POINTS
% of kcals (QCI: 60% of total kcals)	% of carbs as simple carbs	% of carbs as complex carbs	fiber in grams per portion (QCT: 16–24g/day)	% of kcals (QCT: less than 30% of total kcals)	unsat./sat. fat ratio (QCI: at least 2:1)*	cholesterol in mg per portion	EFAs in grams per portion (QCT: at least 5g/day)	max 100
15%	n	n	tr	46%	8.1	59	9.0	65
0%	-	-	0	12%	1.3	49	0.4	53
8%	n	n	tr	43%	2.0	56	0.3	56
18%	1%	99%	0.6	58%	7.9	n	9.8	64
11%	1%	99%	0.2	54%	8.1	n	5.6	61
0%	-	-	0	9%	5.0	88	0.4	59
0%	-	-	0	47%	4.4	9	0.3	50
0%	-	-	0	56%	2.5	52	2.8	58
0%	-	-	0	68%	4.6	84	5.0	61
0%	-	-	0	79%	3.4	158	9.5	61
0%	-	-	0	39%	3.3	14	1.0	54
0%	-	-	0	55%	4.0	60	4.1	63
0%	-	-	0	28%	3.9	18	0.7	53
0%	-	-	0	50%	n	60	n	56
3%	8%	92%	tr	51%	3.3	28	1.7	56
0%	-	-	0	36%	3.4	84	2.0	58
0%	-	-	0	5%	1.5	51	0.2	54
tr	-	-	0	14%	4.5	99	0.5	57
13%	tr	tr	0	23%	2.8	23	0.4	60
0%	-	-	0	9%	2.0	168	0.1	51
30%	14%	86%	0.3	46%	3.3	94	2.4	58
6%	1%	99%	0.1	53%	6.1	378	6.8	65
24%	n	n	0.4	52%	2.8	19	2.8	52
26%	21%	79%	1	42%	0.5	103	0.8	53
3%	1%	99%	tr	94%	11.2	13	8.4	64

*0.5 means half as much unsaturated fat as saturated fat; 2.0 means twice as much

DAIRY PRODUCTS

FOOD	AVERAGE PORTION SIZE	TOTAL CALORIES	PROTEIN CONTENT	
	oz/fl oz per portion	kcals per portion	% of kcals (QCT: 10% of total kcals)	grams per portion (QCT: men 55g/day; women 45g/day)
Milk				
Skim milk	7	64	43%	6.8
Semi-skim (low-fat) milk	7	92	30%	6.8
Whole (full-fat) milk	7	132	20%	6.6
Goat's milk	7	124	20%	6.2
Soy milk, unsweetened	7	52	37%	4.8
Milkshake, thick	7	176	17%	7.4
Cream (2 tbs)				
Light cream	1	58	7%	1.0
Heavy cream	1	149	1%	0.5
Crème fraîche	1	113	2%	0.7
Cheeses				
Brie/camembert	1 ½	137	24%	8.1
Cheddar/Monterey Jack	1 ½	166	24%	10.2
Cottage cheese	1 ½	40	50%	5.0
Cream cheese	1 ½	176	3%	1.2
Edam	1 ½	136	31%	10.7
Feta	1 ½	100	25%	6.2
Goat's cheese, soft	1 ½	128	27%	8.4
Gouda	1 ½	151	27%	10.1
Mozzarella, fresh	1 ½	103	29%	7.4
Parmesan, fresh	1 ½	166	35%	14.5
Stilton	1 ½	164	23%	9.5
Strong blue	1 ½	137	24%	8.2
Yogurt				
Full-fat yogurt, plain	5	119	29%	8.6
Greek-style set yogurt, plain	5	200	17%	8.6
Greek-style yogurt, sheep's milk	5	138	21%	7.2
Soy yogurt, with fruit	5	110	12%	3.2
Fromage frais, plain	3 ½	113	22%	6.1

continues

CARBOHYDRATE CONTENT				FAT CONTENT					QUALITY CALORIE POINTS
% of kcals (QCT: 60% of total kcals)	% of carbs as simple carbs	% of carbs as complex carbs	fiber in grams per portion (QCT: 16–24g/day)	% of kcals (QCT: less than 30% of total kcals)	unsat./sat. fat ratio (QCT: at least 2:1)*	cholesterol in mg per portion	trans fats in grams per portion (QCT: 0)	EFAs in grams per portion (QCT: at least 5g/day)	max 100
51%	100%	0%	0	6%	1.0	6	tr	tr	70
38%	100%	0%	0	32%	0.4	12	0.2	tr	60
26%	100%	0%	0	54%	0.4	28	0.2	0.2	53
27%	100%	0%	0	53%	0.5	22	0.2	0.4	54
7%	100%	0%	tr	56%	7.0	0	tr	2.2	65
65%	97%	3%	tr	18%	0.4	22	0.2	0.2	57
4%	100%	0%	0	89%	0.5	17	0.2	0.2	40
2%	100%	0%	0	97%	0.5	41	0.5	0.6	32
3%	88%	13%	0	95%	0.4	34	0.2	0.3	35
tr	-	-	0	76%	0.4	37	0.5	0.2	37
tr	-	-	0	76%	0.5	39	0.6	0.4	37
12%	100%	0%	0	38%	0.6	6	0.1	0.1	47
tr	-	-	0	97%	0.5	38	n	0.6	34
tr	-	-	0	69%	0.3	28	0.3	0.2	35
2%	100%	0%	0	73%	0.3	28	n	0.2	36
1%	100%	0%	0	72%	0.4	37	0.4	0.4	38
tr	-	-	0	73%	0.4	34	0.4	0.4	37
tr	-	-	0	71%	0.4	23	0.3	0.3	38
1%	100%	0%	0	64%	0.5	37	0.4	0.4	35
0%	-	-	0	77%	0.5	38	0.6	0.5	35
tr	-	-	0	76%	0.4	30	0.4	0.4	38
37%	100%	0%	n	34%	0.6	17	n	0.3	58
14%	94%	6%	0	69%	0.4	26	0.3	0.5	46
20%	100%	0%	0	59%	0.4	21	n	0.3	49
66%	95%	5%	0.5	22%	5.0	0	0	1.7	80
15%	93%	7%	0	63%	0.4	9	0.1	0.2	48

*0.5 means half as much unsaturated fat as saturated fat; 2.0 means twice as much

DAIRY PRODUCTS

FOOD	AVERAGE PORTION SIZE	TOTAL CALORIES	PROTEIN CONTENT	
	oz per portion	kcals per portion	% of kcals (QCT: 10% of total kcals)	grams per portion (QCT: men 55g/day; women 45g/day)
Ice cream				
Dairy ice cream	3 ½	215	7%	3.9
Non-dairy ice cream	3 ½	153	8%	3.0
Eggs and egg dishes				
Egg, boiled	1 ¾	74	34%	6.3
Egg, fried	2	107	30%	8.2
Egg, scrambled	4	308	17%	13.1
Omelet	4	234	22%	13.1
Quiche	4	378	16%	14.9

	CARBOHYDRATE CONTENT				FAT CONTENT				QUALITY CALORIE POINTS
% of kcals (QCT: 60% of total kcals)	% of carbs as simple carbs	% of carbs as complex carbs	fiber in grams per portion (QCT: 16–24g/day)	% of kcals (QCT: less than 30% of total kcals)	unsat./sat. fat ratio (QCT: at least 2:1)*	cholesterol in mg per portion	trans fats in grams per portion (QCT: 0)	EFAs in grams per portion (QCT: at least 5g/day)	max 100
30%	99%	1%	tr	63%	0.5	24	0.7	0.6	32
46%	100%	0%	tr	46%	0.5	n	0.3	0.4	38
tr	-	-	0	66%	1.9	193	.n	0.6	48
tr	-	-	0	70%	1.9	261	n	0.9	37
1%	100%	0%	0	82%	0.8	433	n	2.3	48
tr	-	-	0	78%	1.0	428	n	2.0	36
20%	9%	91%	0.7	64%	1.1	160	0.7	3.8	58

*0.5 means half as much unsaturated fat as saturated fat; 2.0 means twice as much

FATS AND OILS

FOOD	AVERAGE PORTION SIZE	TOTAL CALORIES	PROTEIN CONTENT	
(amounts in brackets represent size of average portion)	oz/fl oz per portion	kcals per portion	% of kcals (QCI: 10% of total kcals)	grams per portion (QCI: men 55g/day; women 45g/day)
Cooking fats (1 tbs)				
Ghee, butter	1/2	135	tr	-
Ghee, vegetable	1/2	134	tr	-
Lard	1/2	134	tr	-
Suet, beef	1/2	124	tr	-
Suet, vegetable	1/2	125	tr	-
Table fats (on 1 slice bread)				
Butter	1/4	74	tr	-
Spread	1/4	68	tr	-
Low-fat spread	1/4	39	7%	-
Margarine, hard	1/4	72	tr	-
- hard vegetable	1/4	74	tr	-
- polyunsaturated	1/4	75	tr	-
Spread (70–80% fat)	1/4	64	tr	-
- (60% fat)	1/4	55	tr	-
- with olive oil	1/4	57	tr	-
- (35–40% fat)	1/4	37	5%	-
- (20–25% fat)	1/4	25	10%	-
Oils (1 tbs)				
Cod liver oil	1/2	135	tr	-
Corn oil	1/2	135	tr	-
Evening primrose oil	1/2	135	tr	-
Grapeseed oil	1/2	135	tr	-
Olive oil	1/2	135	tr	-
Safflower oil	1/2	135	tr	-
Sesame oil	1/2	135	tr	-
Sunflower oil	1/2	135	tr	-
Vegetable oil, blended	1/2	135	tr	-
Walnut oil	1/2	135	tr	-
Wheat germ oil	1/2	135	tr	-

CARBOHYDRATE CONTENT			FAT CONTENT					QUALITY CALORIE POINTS
% of kcals (QCI: 60% of total kcals)	% of carbs as simple carbs	% of carbs as complex carbs	% of kcals (QCI: less than 30% of total kcals)	unsat./sat. fat ratio (QCI: at least 2:1)*	cholesterol in mg per portion	trans fats in grams per portion (QCI: 0)	EFAs in grams per portion (QCI: at least 5g/day)	max 100
tr	-	-	100%	0.4	42	n	0.5	26
tr	-	-	100%	1.0	0	1%	1.5	33
0%	-	-	100%	1.3	14	tr	1.5	33
5%	2%	98%	95%	0.7	12	5%	0.3	30
5%	0%	100%	95%	0.9	0	25%	1.9	35
tr	-	-	100%	0.4	23	4%	0.3	28
1%	100%	0%	99%	1.8	7	13%	0.9	38
tr	-	-	93%	1.1	5	12%	0.7	52
1%	100%	0%	99%	1.2	29	15%	0.5	34
1%	100%	0%	99%	1.2	2	18%	0.9	35
tr	-	-	100%	3.7	tr	8%	3.6	58
tr	-	-	100%	4.3	tr	4%	3.3	50
1%	100%	0%	99%	4.1	tr	5%	2.9	50
1%	100%	0%	99%	4.3	0	10%	1.3	45
2%	68%	32%	93%	3.1	tr	2%	1.8	50
4%	99%	1%	86%	2.7	1	10%	0.5	51
0%	-	-	100%	3.7	86	tr	4.5	48
0%	-	-	100%	5.6	0	tr	7.7	54
0%	-	-	100%	11.2	0	tr	11.5	58
0%	-	-	100%	7.6	0	tr	10.2	54
0%	-	-	100%	5.7	0	tr	1.2	42
0%	-	-	100%	8.9	0	tr	11.1	57
0%	-	-	100%	5.5	0	tr	6.5	52
0%	-	-	100%	7.0	0	tr	9.5	55
0%	-	-	100%	8.0	0	tr	7.2	54
0%	-	-	100%	9.5	0	tr	10.5	56
0%	-	-	100%	4.1	0	tr	9.1	53

*0.5 means half as much unsaturated fat as saturated fat; 2.0 means twice as much

GRAINS, CEREALS, BREADS

FOOD	AVERAGE PORTION SIZE	TOTAL CALORIES	PROTEIN CONTENT	
	oz per portion	kcals per portion	% of kcals (QCT: 10% of total kcals)	grams per portion (QCT: men 55g/day; women 45g/day)
Flours and grains				
Barley, pearl	3 ½	360	9%	7.9
Buckwheat	3 ½	364	9%	8.1
Bulgur wheat	3 ½	353	11%	9.7
Cornstarch	3 ½	354	1%	0.6
Couscous	3 ½	227	10%	5.7
Custard powder	3 ½	354	1%	0.6
Millet	3 ½	354	7%	5.8
Oatmeal	3 ½	401	12%	12.4
Quinoa	3 ½	309	18%	13.8
Rice, brown	7	282	7%	5.2
Rice, white	7	276	8%	5.2
Rice flour	3 ½	366	7%	6.4
Rye flour	3 ½	335	10%	8.2
Soy flour	3 ½	447	33%	36.8
Wheat flour, white	3 ½	341	11%	9.4
Wheat flour, wholewheat	3 ½	310	16%	12.7
Wheat germ	¾	76	35%	6.7
Wheat bran	½	31	27%	2.1
Noodles and pasta (cooked)				
Noodles, egg	10	186	14%	6.6
Noodles, plain	10	186	15%	7.2
Pasta, white	10	312	14%	10.8
Pasta, wholewheat	10	339	17%	14.1
Pastry				
Puff pastry	3 ½	373	6%	5.7
Shortcrust pastry	3 ½	449	5%	5.7
Breakfast cereals				
All-bran	1 ¾	126	24%	7.6
Coco pops	1 ¾	193	5%	2.7

continues

	CARBOHYDRATE CONTENT				FAT CONTENT			QUALITY CALORIE POINTS
% of kcals (QCT: 60% of total kcals)	% of carbs as simple carbs	% of carbs as complex carbs	fiber in grams per portion (QCT: 16–24g/day)	% of kcals (QCT: less than 30% of total kcals)	unsat./sat. fat ratio (QCT: at least 2:1)*	cholesterol in mg per portion	EFAs in grams per portion (QCT: at least 5g/day)	max 100
87%	tr	100%	5.9	4%	3.1	0	0.8	75
87%	tr	100%	2.1	4%	n	0	n	71
81%	n	n	n	8%	n	0	n	74
97%	tr	100%	0.1	2%	4.9	0	0.3	65
85%	n	n	n	5%	n	0	n	75
97%	tr	100%	0.1	2%	n	0	n	64
79%	n	n	n	14%	n	0	n	72
68%	tr	100%	6.3	20%	4.4	0	3.5	87
67%	11%	89%	5.3	15%	n	0	n	85
86%	2%	98%	7.6	7%	n	0	n	90
84%	tr	100%	3.0	8%	3.2	0	0.2	76
82%	100%	0%	2.0	11%	n	0	n	72
85%	100%	0%	11.7	5%	4.3	0	1.0	83
20%	48%	52%	11.2	47%	2.7	0	3.3	79
85%	2%	98%	3.1	4%	4.1	0	0.5	74
78%	3%	97%	9.0	6%	3.9	0	0.9	85
56%	36%	64%	3.9	9%	n	0	n	95
49%	14%	86%	5.9	24%	3.9	0	0.4	78
79%	2%	98%	3.0	7%	1.2	90	1.8	70
79%	2%	98%	3.6	6%	n	0	n	83
80%	2%	98%	5.4	6%	3.8	0	0.4	79
77%	6%	94%	12.0	6%	n	0	n	89
37%	2%	98%	2.3	57%	n	57	n	62
39%	2%	98%	2.2	56%	1.4	11	3.5	63
64%	36%	64%	15.0	12%	3.9	0	1.5	87
92%	41%	59%	0.6	3%	n	0	n	42

*0.5 means half as much unsaturated fat as saturated fat; 2.0 means twice as much

GRAINS, CEREALS, BREADS

FOOD	AVERAGE PORTION SIZE	TOTAL CALORIES	PROTEIN CONTENT	
(where appropriate, numbers in brackets represent number of items in average portion)	oz per portion	kcals per portion	% of kcals (QCI: 10% of total kcals)	grams per portion (QCI: men 55g/day; women 45g/day)
Corn flakes	1 ³/₄	178	9%	4.0
Fruit 'n' Fibre	1 ³/₄	176	9%	4.1
Grapenuts	1 ³/₄	173	12%	5.3
Muesli (Swiss style)	2 ¹/₂	255	12%	7.4
Porridge (made with water)	7	98	12%	3.0
Puffed wheat	1 ³/₄	161	18%	7.1
Rice Krispies	1 ³/₄	185	7%	3.1
Shredded wheat (2)	1 ³/₄	163	13%	5.3
Special K	1 ³/₄	190	16%	7.7
Weetabix (2)	1 ¹/₂	142	12%	4.3
Breads and rolls				
Bagel (1)	3 ¹/₄	246	15%	9.0
Brown bread (1 slice)	1 ¹/₂	87	16%	3.4
Chapati (1)	2	111	14%	4.0
French stick (2 in slice)	1 ¹/₂	108	14%	3.8
Granary bread (1 slice)	1 ¹/₂	94	16%	3.7
Naan bread (1)	5 ¹/₂	538	11%	14.2
Papadum (fried) (2)	³/₄	96	19%	4.6
Pita bread (1 large)	3 ¹/₂	252	14%	8.7
Rye bread (1 slice)	³/₄	55	15%	2.1
Wheat germ bread (1 slice)	1 ¹/₂	105	14%	3.7
White bread (1 slice)	1 ¹/₂	94	14%	3.4
Wholewheat bread (1 slice)	1 ¹/₂	86	17%	3.7
Croissant (1)	1 ³/₄	180	9%	4.2
Hamburger bun (1)	1 ³/₄	132	14%	4.6
Soft white roll (1)	1 ³/₄	135	15%	5.2
Wholewheat roll (1)	1 ³/₄	121	15%	4.5

	CARBOHYDRATE CONTENT					FAT CONTENT			QUALITY CALORIE POINTS
% of kcals (QCT: 60% of total kcals)	% of carbs as simple carbs	% of carbs as complex carbs	fiber in grams per portion (QCT: 16–24g/day)	% of kcals (QCT: less than 30% of total kcals)	unsat./sat. fat ratio (QCT: at least 2:1)*	cholesterol in mg per portion	EFAs in grams per portion (QCT: at least 5g/day)		max 100
90%	8%	92%	1.7	1%	5.0	0	0.4		69
78%	37%	63%	5.1	13%	n	0	n		74
87%	15%	85%	3.1	1%	n	0	n		73
73%	33%	67%	5.7	15%	4.4	0	2.1		79
69%	tr	100%	1.6	19%	4.9	0	0.7		73
79%	tr	100%	4.4	4%	4.2	0	0.3		69
91%	12%	88%	0.6	2%	2.6	0	0.4		69
78%	1%	99%	5.1	8%	3.8	0	0.7		75
82%	22%	78%	1.4	2%	n	0	n		72
83%	8%	92%	3.4	5%	3.8	0	0.6		73
79%	11%	89%	2.2	6%	n	0	n		71
76%	7%	93%	2.4	8%	2.9	0	0.4		74
82%	4%	96%	3.5	4%	4.3	0	0.3		75
77%	3%	97%	2.0	9%	n	0	-		71
74%	5%	95%	2.6	10%	n	0	n		75
56%	11%	89%	3.5	33%	n	14	n		72
40%	0%	100%	2.4	41%	n	0	n		53
82%	4%	96%	3.7	4%	n	0	n		72
79%	4%	96%	1.5	6%	n	0	n		73
61%	6%	94%	2.2	25%	n	0	n		75
79%	5%	95%	1.5	7%	2.3	0	0.3		70
73%	4%	96%	3.0	10%	2.9	0	0.5		75
40%	3%	97%	1.3	51%	n	26	n		61
69%	5%	95%	2.0	17%	n	0	n		71
75%	4%	96%	2.1	10%	2.2	0	0.6		71
75%	3%	97%	4.4	10%	2.9	0	0.7		76

*0.5 means half as much unsaturated fat as saturated fat; 2.0 means twice as much

BISCUITS, CAKES, DESSERTS

FOOD	AVERAGE PORTION SIZE	TOTAL CALORIES	PROTEIN CONTENT	
(where appropriate, numbers in brackets represent number of items in average portion)	oz per portion	kcals per portion	% of kcals (QCT: 10% of total kcals)	grams per portion (QCT: men 55g/day; women 45g/day)
Biscuits and cookies				
Chocolate cookie (1)	¾	131	4%	1.4
Cream cracker (1)	½	66	9%	1.4
Crispbread, rye (1)	½	32	12%	0.9
Flapjack (oatmeal cookie) (1)	2	290	4%	2.7
Graham cracker (1)	½	71	5%	0.9
Oatcake (1)	½	66	9%	1.5
Plain cookie (1)	½	46	6%	0.7
Plain cracker (1)	½	44	10%	1.1
Shortbread (1)	½	75	5%	0.9
Wholewheat cookie (1)	½	54	15%	2.0
Wholewheat cracker (1)	½	62	10%	1.5
Cakes				
Chocolate cake (1 slice)	2 ½	319	6%	5.2
Fruit cake (1 slice)	2 ½	248	6%	3.6
Gâteau (1 slice)	2 ½	236	7%	4.0
Sponge cake (1 slice)	2 ½	321	6%	4.5
Jelly roll (1 slice)	1 ¼	97	10%	2.5
Desserts				
Cheesecake (1 slice)	3 ¾	452	5%	5.9
Christmas pudding	3 ½	291	6%	4.6
Fruit crisp/cobbler	6	337	4%	3.4
Custard sauce (made with milk)	5	176	13%	5.6
Fruit pie	4	223	4%	2.4
Pancake (1)	3 ¾	331	8%	6.5
Rice pudding	7	178	15%	6.8
Trifle	6	272	9%	6.1
Buns and pastries				
Crumpet (1)	1 ½	71	14%	2.4
Currant bun (1)	2	178	10%	4.6

continues

CARBOHYDRATE CONTENT				FAT CONTENT				QUALITY CALORIE POINTS
% of kcals (QCT: 60% of total kcals)	% of carbs as simple carbs	% of carbs as complex carbs	fiber in grams per portion (QCT: 16–24g/day)	% of kcals (QCT: less than 30% of total kcals)	unsat./sat. fat ratio (QCT: at least 2:1)*	cholesterol in mg per portion	EFAs in grams per portion (QCT: at least 5g/day)	max 100
49%	64%	36%	0.7	47%	0.6	n	0.3	32
58%	tr	100%	0.9	33%	n	n	n	61
82%	5%	95%	1.2	6%	4.1	0	0.1	72
47%	59%	41%	1.6	49%	n	n	n	36
55%	20%	80%	0.7	40%	n	3	n	39
54%	5%	95%	0.5	37%	3.4	0	0.8	71
61%	30%	70%	0.2	33%	1.0	0	0.2	42
64%	3%	97%	0.6	26%	n	0	n	63
48%	27%	73%	0.3	47%	0.6	11	0.2	33
63%	8%	92%	1.2	22%	n	0	n	63
65%	2%	98%	0.7	25%	n	0	n	67
42%	57%	43%	2.7	52%	0.5	85	0.6	31
61%	74%	26%	1.8	33%	1.6	37	1.2	49
48%	74%	26%	0.4	45%	n	116	n	38
42%	58%	42%	0.7	52%	1.6	90	2.7	41
76%	74%	26%	0.4	14%	n	66	n	46
23%	55%	45%	0.8	72%	0.8	120	2.3	26
64%	69%	31%	2.7	30%	1.0	49	0.7	43
64%	63%	37%	3.7	32%	1.6	n	1.9	53
52%	69%	31%	n	35%	0.6	24	0.2	41
58%	54%	46%	0.5	38%	n	4	n	45
43%	46%	54%	1.0	49%	1.1	80	1.6	42
59%	59%	41%	0.4	26%	n	30	n	49
52%	75%	25%	0.7	39%	1.0	85	0.7	43
81%	4%	96%	1.0	5%	n	0	n	66
67%	29%	71%	1.1	23%	n	10	n	44

*0.5 means half as much unsaturated fat as saturated fat; 2.0 means twice as much

BISCUITS, CAKES, DESSERTS

FOOD	AVERAGE PORTION SIZE	TOTAL CALORIES	PROTEIN CONTENT	
(where appropriate, numbers in brackets represent number of items in average portion)	oz per portion	kcals per portion	% of kcals (QCT: 10% of total kcals)	grams per portion (QCT: men 55g/day; women 45g/day)
Danish pastry (1)	3 ¾	411	6%	6.4
Doughnut (jelly) (1)	2 ½	252	7%	4.3
Greek pastry (Baklava) (1)	3 ½	322	6%	4.7
Hot cross bun (1)	1 ¾	155	10%	3.7
Muffin (American) (1)	2 ½	256	7%	4.4
Muffin (English) (1)	2 ½	198	14%	7.1
Scone (1)	1 ¾	181	8%	3.6
Teacake (1)	2	178	11%	4.8
Waffle (1)	2 ¼	217	10%	5.7

| CARBOHYDRATE CONTENT | | | | FAT CONTENT | | | | QUALITY CALORIE POINTS |
% of kcals (QCI: 60% of total kcals)	% of carbs as simple carbs	% of carbs as complex carbs	fiber in grams per portion (QCI: 16–24g/day)	% of kcals (QCI: less than 30% of total kcals)	unsat./sat. fat ratio (QCI: at least 2:1)*	cholesterol in mg per portion	EFAs in grams per portion (QCI: at least 5g/day)	max 100
52%	56%	44%	3.0	42%	n	45	n	**40**
54%	39%	61%	1.9	39%	n	11	n	**42**
46%	46%	54%	1.9	48%	n	n	n	**39**
70%	40%	60%	1.1	20%	n	13	n	**44**
54%	54%	46%	1.1	39%	0.6	48	0.6	**57**
66%	5%	95%	1.9	20%	n	21	n	**47**
56%	11%	89%	1.1	36%	1.5	3	1.1	**46**
66%	28%	72%	2.5	23%	n	11	n	**46**
45%	9%	91%	1.3	45%	n	79	n	**49**

*0.5 means half as much unsaturated fat as saturated fat; 2.0 means twice as much

SUGAR PRODUCTS

FOOD	AVERAGE PORTION SIZE	TOTAL CALORIES	PROTEIN CONTENT	
(where appropriate, numbers in brackets represent size of average portion)	oz per portion	kcals per portion	% of kcals (QCT: 10% of total kcals)	grams per portion (QCT: men 55g/day; women 45g/day)
Sugars and syrups (1 tbs)				
Honey	½	58	1%	0.1
Molasses	½	53	0%	0
Sugar, brown	½	72	tr	tr
Sugar, white	½	79	tr	tr
Syrup, light corn	½	60	tr	tr
Syrup, maple	½	52	0%	0
Treacle, black	½	51	2%	0.2
Preserves and spreads (1 tbs)				
Chocolate nut spread	½	110	5%	1.2
Fruit spread	½	24	3%	0.1
Jelly	½	52	1%	0.1
Chocolate				
Chocolate bar	1 ¾	221	5%	2.7
Milk chocolate	1 ¾	260	6%	3.9
Plain chocolate	1 ¾	255	4%	2.5
Confectionery				
Hard candy	1 ¾	164	tr	tr
Cereal crunchy bar	1 ¾	234	9%	5.2
Fruit pastilles	1 ¾	164	3%	1.4
Halva (with carrot)	1 ¾	177	5%	2.3
Liquorice shapes	1 ¾	139	8%	2.8
Nougat	1 ¾	192	5%	2.2
Peppermints	1 ¾	197	1%	0.3
Turkish delight (with nuts)	1 ¾	172	5%	2.1

CARBOHYDRATE CONTENT					FAT CONTENT			QUALITY CALORIE POINTS
% of kcals (QCT: 60% of total kcals)	% of carbs as simple carbs	% of carbs as complex carbs	fiber in grams per portion (QCT: 16–24g/day)	% of kcals (QCT: less than 30% of total kcals)	unsat./sat. fat ratio (QCT: at least 2:1)*	cholesterol in mg per portion	EFAs in grams per portion (QCT: at least 5g/day)	max 100
98%	100%	0%	0	1%	-	0	0	31
97%	100%	0%	tr	3%	-	0	tr	30
100%	100%	0%	0	0%	-	0	0	29
100%	100%	0%	0	0%	-	0	0	28
99%	100%	0%	0	1%	-	0	0	29
96%	100%	0%	tr	4%	-	0	tr	31
98%	100%	0%	0	0%	-	0	0	32
41%	99%	1%	0.2	54%	2.1	tr	0.9	39
97%	98%	2%	n	0%	-	0	0	36
99%	100%	0%	0.2	0%	-	0	0	33
56%	99%	1%	n	39%	0.8	13	0.4	37
41%	99%	1%	0.4	53%	0.6	12	0.6	30
47%	98%	2%	1.3	49%	0.6	0	0.5	33
100%	100%	0%	0	0%	-	0	0	29
48%	53%	47%	n	43%	3.7	tr	2.7	53
97%	96%	4%	n	0%	-	0	0	31
47%	99%	1%	1.5	48%	0.6	25	0.7	37
88%	69%	31%	n	4%	n	0	n	37
75%	99%	1%	n	20%	6.3	0	1.4	42
98%	100%	0%	0	1%	n	0	n	30
88%	100%	0%	0.2	7%	7.0	0	0.4	47

*0.5 means half as much unsaturated fat as saturated fat; 2.0 means twice as much

SOUPS AND SAUCES

FOOD	AVERAGE PORTION SIZE	TOTAL CALORIES	PROTEIN CONTENT	
	fl oz per portion	kcals per portion	% of kcals (QCI: 10% of total kcals)	grams per portion (QCI: men 55g/day; women 45g/day)
Soups (1 cup)				
Bouillabaisse	9	338	31%	26.0
Carrot and orange soup	9	50	8%	1.0
Chicken soup	9	145	12%	4.3
French onion soup	9	100	2%	0.5
Gazpacho	9	113	7%	2.0
Leek and potato soup	9	130	12%	3.8
Lentil soup	9	293	19%	14.0
Minestrone soup	9	158	11%	4.5
Mushroom soup	9	115	10%	2.8
Oxtail soup	9	110	22%	6.0
Tomato soup	9	130	6%	2.0
Vegetable soup	9	130	7%	2.3
Sauces				
Black bean sauce	1	28	31%	2.1
Brown sauce (spicy)	1	36	4%	0.4
Curry sauce	4	90	8%	1.7
Dressing, Thousand Island	1	97	1%	0.3
Dressing, yogurt-based	1	88	3%	0.7
Gravy (instant)	2 ½	24	4%	0.2
Hollandaise sauce	2 ½	495	3%	3.4
Mayonnaise	1	207	1%	0.3
Mint sauce	½	10	6%	0.2
Raita	1 ¾	29	30%	2.2
Soy sauce	½	4	28%	0.3
Sweet and sour sauce	5	66	4%	0.6
Tomato ketchup	1	35	6%	0.5
Vinaigrette	1	139	tr	tr

	CARBOHYDRATE CONTENT				FAT CONTENT			QUALITY CALORIE POINTS
% of kcals (QCT: 60% of total kcals)	% of carbs as simple carbs	% of carbs as complex carbs	fiber in grams per portion (QCT: 16–24g/day)	% of kcals (QCT: less than 30% of total kcals)	unsat./sat. fat ratio (QCT: at least 2:1)*	cholesterol in mg per portion	EFAs in grams per portion (QCT: at least 5g/day)	max 100
4%	94%	6%	1.0	65%	5.6	80	2.3	55
69%	95%	5%	2.8	23%	2.0	0	0.3	75
29%	24%	76%	tr	59%	5.0	243	2.5	62
53%	100%	0%	3.3	45%	8.5	0	2.5	80
22%	96%	4%	n	71%	5.6	0	0.8	66
44%	24%	76%	4.5	44%	3.0	0	0.5	75
45%	14%	86%	6.3	36%	9.2	0	2.5	82
46%	18%	82%	1.5	43%	0.8	5	0.3	61
31%	21%	79%	0.3	59%	5.0	0	2.3	68
43%	18%	82%	0.3	35%	1.3	18	0.5	62
43%	44%	56%	1.8	51%	4.8	0	2.0	71
23%	56%	44%	2.8	70%	5.8	0	2.0	66
49%	91%	9%	0.6	20%	n	0	n	49
87%	87%	13%	0.2	9%	n	0	n	42
34%	52%	48%	n	58%	n	0	n	34
15%	86%	14%	0.1	84%	n	9	n	24
9%	75%	25%	n	88%	n	n	n	46
33%	3%	97%	tr	63%	n	n	n	34
tr	-	-	tr	97%	0.5	340	2.2	29
1%	76%	24%	0	98%	5.4	39	2.2	25
80%	100%	0%	n	14%	n	0	tr	45
37%	99%	1%	0.1	33%	0.6	4	0.1	46
71%	89%	11%	0	1%	0	0	0	36
90%	69%	31%	n	6%	n	0	0	42
93%	96%	4%	0.3	1%	n	0	tr	42
4%	100%	0 %	0	96%	n	0	n	36

*0.5 means half as much unsaturated fat as saturated fat; 2.0 means twice as much

PICKLES AND SAVOURIES

FOOD	AVERAGE PORTION SIZE	TOTAL CALORIES	PROTEIN CONTENT	
(where appropriate, numbers in brackets represent number of items in average portion)	oz per portion	kcals per portion	% of kcals (QCT: 10% of total kcals)	grams per portion (QCT: men 55g/day; women 45g/day)
Pickles and chutneys				
Lime pickle	1 ½	71	4%	0.8
Piccalilli	1 ½	34	5%	0.4
Relish (corn/cucumber/onion)	1 ½	48	3%	0.4
Sweet mango chutney	1 ½	76	2%	0.3
Tomato chutney	1 ½	51	4%	0.5
Tomatoes, sun-dried	1 ¾	248	3%	1.7
Savoury snacks				
Breadsticks (grissini) (3)	¾	78	11%	2.2
Popcorn, plain	1 ¾	297	4%	3.1
Potato chips	1 ½	212	4%	2.3
Potato chips, low-fat	1 ½	183	6%	2.6
Pretzels	1 ¾	191	10%	4.6
Tortilla chips	1 ¾	230	7%	3.8

	CARBOHYDRATE CONTENT				FAT CONTENT			QUALITY CALORIE POINTS
% of kcals (QCT: 60% of total kcals)	% of carbs as simple carbs	% of carbs as complex carbs	fiber in grams per portion (QCT: 16–24g/day)	% of kcals (QCT: less than 30% of total kcals)	unsat./sat. fat ratio (QCT: at least 2:1)*	cholesterol in mg per portion	EFAs in grams per portion (QCT: at least 5g/day)	max 100
18%	n	n	2.2	78%	n	0	n	34
78%	84%	16%	0.8	17%	4.0	0	0.1	50
92%	88%	12%	0.5	5%	n	0	0.1	43
96%	94%	6%	n	2%	n	0	tr	44
91%	91%	9%	0.5	5%	n	0	tr	50
4%	54%	46%	n	93%	6.3	0	13.6	63
70%	7%	93%	0.6	19%	0.4	0	0.2	50
31%	2%	98%	n	65%	8.0	0	9.9	52
38%	1%	99%	4.3	58%	1.0	0	2.0	36
52%	2%	98%	5.5	42%	1.2	0	1.0	44
78%	n	n	n	12%	3.3	0	0.6	46
49%	2%	98%	3.0	44%	4.3	0	3.4	54

*0.5 means half as much unsaturated fat as saturated fat; 2.0 means twice as much

DRINKS

FOOD	AVERAGE PORTION SIZE	TOTAL CALORIES	ALCOHOL CONTENT	PROTEIN CONTENT	
(where appropriate, numbers in brackets represent size of average portion)	fl oz per portion	kcals per portion	% of kcals	% of kcals (QCT: 10% of total kcals)	grams per portion (QCT: men 55g/day; women 45g/day)
Fruit juices (unsweetened)					
Apple juice	7	76	0%	1%	0.2
Cranberry juice	7	122	0%	0%	tr
Grape juice	7	92	0%	3%	0.6
Grapefruit juice	7	66	0%	5%	0.8
Lemon juice (2 tsp)	3/4	1	0%	17%	0.1
Lime juice (2 tsp)	3/4	2	0%	18%	0.1
Mango juice	7	78	0%	1%	0.2
Orange juice	7	66	0%	7%	1.2
Passionfruit juice	7	94	0%	7%	1.6
Pineapple juice	7	82	0%	3%	0.6
Pomegranate juice	7	88	0%	2%	0.4
Prune juice	7	114	0%	4%	1.0
Hot drinks					
Coffee, black	7	4	0%	40%	0.4
Coffee, with milk	7	13	0%	29%	1.0
Coffee, Irish	7	160	43%	2%	0.8
Drinking chocolate (for 1 mug)	1/2	66	0%	6%	1.0
Tea, black	7	tr	0%	tr	tr
Tea, with milk	7	15	0%	20%	0.8
Tea, green	7	tr	0%	tr	tr
Tea, herbal	7	2	0%	0%	0
Soft drinks (carbonated)					
Cola	11	129	0%	tr	n
Fruit juice drink	11	129	0%	tr	n
Ginger beer	9	38	0%	0%	0
Lemonade	7	44	0%	tr	tr
Sports drinks	7	120	0%	tr	tr
Tonic water	9	83	0%	0%	0

continues

	CARBOHYDRATE CONTENT					FAT CONTENT			QUALITY CALORIE POINTS
% of kcals (QCT: 60% of total kcals)	% of carbs as simple carbs	% of carbs as complex carbs	fiber in grams per portion (QCT: 16–24g/day)	% of kcals (QCT: less than 30% of total kcals)	unsat./sat. fat ratio (QCT: at least 2:1)*	cholesterol in mg per portion	EFAs in grams per portion (QCT: at least 5g/day)		max 100
98%	100%	0%	tr	1%	n	0	n		69
100%	n	n	n	0%	n	0	0		75
95%	100%	0%	0	2%	n	0	n		69
94%	100%	0%	tr	1%	n	0	n		71
83%	100%	0%	tr	tr	n	0	n		74
76%	100%	0%	tr	6%	n	0	n		75
94%	98%	2%	tr	5%	n	0	n		72
92%	100%	0%	0.2	1%	n	0	n		73
85%	100%	0%	tr	8%	n	0	n		76
96%	100%	0%	tr	1%	n	0	n		70
97%	100%	0%	tr	1%	n	0	n		70
94%	100%	0%	tr	2%	n	0	n		70
56%	100%	0%	0	4%	n	0	tr		59
26%	100%	0%	0	45%	0.3	4	tr		51
14%	100%	0%	0	41%	0.5	40	0.4		32
79%	95%	5%	0	15%	n	n	n		41
tr	-	-	0	tr	n	0	n		57
23%	100%	0%	0	57%	n	4	tr		50
tr	-	-	0	tr	n	0	0		69
75%	n	n	0	25%	n	0	tr		70
99%	100%	0%	0	tr	n	0	0		45
99%	100%	0%	0	tr	n	tr	0		46
99%	100%	0%	0	0%	0	0	0		45
100%	100%	0%	0	0%	0	0	0		45
100%	99%	1%	0	0%	0	0	0		47
100%	100%	0%	0	0%	0	0	0		47

*0.5 means half as much unsaturated fat as saturated fat; 2.0 means twice as much

DRINKS

FOOD	AVERAGE PORTION SIZE	TOTAL CALORIES	ALCOHOL CONTENT	PROTEIN CONTENT	
	fl oz per portion	kcals per portion	% of kcals	% of kcals (QCT: 10% of total kcals)	grams per portion (QCT: men 55g/day; women 45g/day)
Soft drinks (uncarbonated)					
Barley water (diluted)	7	28	0%	3%	0.2
Fruit juice drink (diluted)	7	74	0%	1%	0.2
Rosehip syrup (diluted)	7	92	0%	0%	0
Alcoholic drinks					
Beer, dark	10	177	68%	4%	0.9
Beer, lager	10	384	96%	4%	0.9
Beer, shandy	10	48	30%	tr	tr
Beer, stout (eg. Guinness)	10	156	77%	5%	1.2
Cider	10	108	73%	tr	tr
Champagne	4 ½	95	91%	2%	0.4
Red wine	4 ½	85	98%	1%	0.1
White wine	4 ½	83	96%	1%	0.1
Port	2	79	71%	0%	0.1
Sherry	2	58	94%	1%	0.1
Vermouth/martini	2	55	90%	tr	tr
Cream liqueurs (eg. Kahlua)	¾	81	29%	tr	tr
Liqueurs, high-strength (eg. Grand Marnier)	¾	79	71%	tr	tr
Liqueurs, med.-strength (eg. campari)	¾	66	53%	tr	tr
Spirits (eg. brandy/gin/whiskey)	¾	56	100%	tr	tr

	CARBOHYDRATE CONTENT					FAT CONTENT			QUALITY CALORIE POINTS
% of kcals (QCT: 60% of total kcals)	% of carbs as simple carbs	% of carbs as complex carbs	fiber in grams per portion (QCT: 16–24g/day)	% of kcals (QCT: less than 30% of total kcals)	unsat./sat. fat ratio (QCT: at least 2:1)*	cholesterol in mg per portion	EFAs in grams per portion (QCT: at least 5g/day)	max 100
97%	100%	0%	tr	tr	0	0	0	47
99%	100%	0%	tr	0%	0	0	0	46
100%	100%	0%	0	0%	0	0	0	47
27%	100%	0%	tr	1%	tr	tr	0	32
tr	-	-	tr	tr	tr	tr	0	21
70%	100%	0%	tr	0%	0	0	0	37
18%	100%	0%	tr	tr	tr	0	tr	31
27%	100%	0%	0	0%	0	0	0	33
7%	100%	0%	0	0%	0	0	0	29
1%	100%	0%	0	0%	0	0	0	27
3%	100%	0%	0	0%	0	0	0	28
29%	100%	0%	0	0%	0	0	0	32
5%	100%	0%	0	0%	0	0	0	28
10%	100%	0%	0	0%	0	0	0	28
26%	100%	0%	0	45%	n	n	n	19
29%	100%	0%	0	0%	0	0	0	30
47%	100%	0%	0	0%	0	0	0	34
tr	-	-	0	0%	0	0	0	25

*0.5 means half as much unsaturated fat as saturated fat; 2.0 means twice as much

Part 3
VITAMINS, MINERALS, & TRACE ELEMENTS

In this section we explore the main vitamins, minerals, and trace elements that are essential to health. We look at the foods in which they can be found, how they are used within the body, the causes and symptoms of deficiency, and the effects of excessive intakes. For each nutrient there is also a box that specifies the recommended daily intake and lists the top ten foods containing that nutrient. This is followed by nutritional tables, which detail the amounts of vitamins, minerals, and trace elements present in a range of foods. Using this information you can create a healthy diet that is high in essential nutrients.

All about vitamins

Fat-soluble vitamins

VITAMIN A

Vitamin A is a family of chemicals that includes retinol (derived from animal sources), and about 50 different carotenoids (derived from plant foods). The most common carotenoid is beta-carotene, which is found in abundance in carrots, green leaves, and peppers. Other important carotenoids include alpha-carotene, gamma-carotene and beta-cryptoxanthin.

About one sixth of the carotenoids we eat are converted into retinol in the body and stored in the liver, fat tissues, lungs, testicles, bone marrow, eyes, and kidneys. Vitamin A is important for good vision, skin, reproduction, pregnancy, growth, and immunity, and also protects against bacterial, parasitic, and viral infections. In addition, carotenoids are powerful antioxidants that help us resist cancer and heart disease.

The average adult needs about 800 micrograms of retinol or 4800 micrograms of beta-carotene per day. Vitamin A is found in many different foods and deficiency is rare in affluent societies, but during illness, and in cases of fat malabsorption, extra vitamin A (carotenoids in particular) is needed in the diet.

In poorer countries, vitamin A deficiency is a major health problem with more than 200 million children affected worldwide due to poverty, disease, and severe shortages of fresh food. Vitamin A deficiency causes decreased immunity and, in severe cases, eye disease and blindness.

Taking supplements has been shown to be ineffective in the treatment of vitamin A deficiency because of problems with absorption from the digestive tract. Carotenoids in foods are well-absorbed, however. Consuming a lot of carotenoid-rich food may tint the skin yellow, but does not cause toxicity. By contrast, too much retinol can cause bone and liver damage and, in pregnancy, may harm the developing baby. Signs of retinol toxicity include headache, blurred vision, vomiting, and vertigo.

Vitamin A TOP 10 (micrograms per 100 grams of food)

BETA-CAROTENE
FDA recommended intake = 4800 µg/day
Toxicity level = none

1.	paprika	36250	6.	red pepper	3780
2.	carrots	12472	7.	spinach	3535
3.	sweet potato	8910	8.	curly kale	3145
4.	beet greens	8295	9.	watercress	2520
5.	parsley	4040	10.	canteloup melon	1765

RETINOL
FDA recommended intake = 700–900 µg/day
Upper tolerable limit = 3000 µg/day

1.	cod liver oil	18000	6.	margarine	
2.	liver	17300		(on average)	665
3.	liver pâté	7300	7.	crème fraîche	388
4.	butter	958	8.	cheese (on average)	300
5.	double cream	779	9.	eggs	190
			10.	greek-style yogurt	115

VITAMIN D

At the beginning of the 20th century, a bone disease called rickets was rife among poor children in northern industrialized countries. It was cured—and prevented—with cod liver oil, and research revealed that this effect could be reproduced by two chemicals, cholecalciferol (Vitamin D3, found in animal tissues) and ergocalciferol (Vitamin D2, produced from plant sterols).

Many foods are now fortified with vitamin D, but sunlight is our most important source because it triggers vitamin D production in the skin. Just one hour a day of sunlight on a small patch of skin is enough, and during the summer the body produces and stores plenty to last the winter.

Vitamin D enhances calcium absorption and influences its uptake and release from bones. Deficiency causes stunted growth, bone pain and deformity, dental and nerve problems, muscle weakness, anemia, and a predisposition to respiratory infections. Too much dietary vitamin D causes abnormally high levels of calcium in the blood, leading to serious health problems, such as kidney damage. Symptoms of toxicity include loss of appetite, nausea, diarrhea, muscle weakness, and joint pain.

As most of us get sufficient vitamin D from the action of sunlight on our skin, a dietary intake is only vital for pregnant women, nursing mothers, and those who are rarely exposed to sunlight, such as the housebound, the elderly, women following strict religious dress codes, submariners, and astronauts.

Vitamin D TOP 10 (micrograms per 100 grams of food)

CHOLECALCIFEROL

FDA recommended intakes = 0 μg/day if adequate exposure to
sunlight; 5 μg/day if no sun exposure; 10–15 μg/day for over-50s.
Toxicity level = >50 μg/day

1.	cod liver oil	210.0	6.	kipper, mackerel	8.0
2.	herring	19.0	7.	salmon	7.1
3.	cod roe	17.0	8.	sardines, tuna	4.1
4.	trout	9.6	9.	eggs	1.8
5.	butter, lard,		10.	corned beef,	
	margarine	8.2		liver pâté	1.3

VITAMIN E

Vitamin E (also known as tocopherol) is a major antioxidant,
which stabilizes cell membranes and protects them against
damage from free radicals and environmental toxins. It also
inhibits the production of the inflammatory prostaglandins that
cause many of the symptoms of autoimmune diseases such as
rheumatoid arthritis. It plays a role in the synthesis of DNA, and
is thought to protect against heart disease and cancer.

Vitamin E is found in a wide variety of foods so deficiency
is uncommon. However, since vitamin E has important effects

on immune function, there is a distinction between the amount needed to avoid dietary deficiency and the amount needed to help prevent disease. Higher intakes (50 mg per day) can decrease the risk of immune-related conditions, and help prevent or delay the development of Parkinson's disease and other degenerative neurological disorders such as multiple sclerosis. Vitamin E is also thought to reduce the risk of cataracts, arthritis, and chronic fatigue syndrome.

Vitamin E deficiency leads to cell membrane damage, which in turn causes muscle, nerve, and liver dysfunction. As tobacco smoke contains large amounts of free radicals,

Vitamin E TOP 10 (milligrams per 100 grams of food)

TOCOPHEROL
FDA recommended intake = 15 mg/day
Upper tolerable limit = 1000 mg/day

1.	wheat germ oil	136.7	6.	almonds, hazelnuts	24.5
2.	sunflower oil	49.2	7.	sun-dried tomatoes	24.0
3.	safflower oil	40.7	8.	wheat germ	22.0
4.	sunflower seeds	37.8	9.	cod liver oil	20.0
5.	polyunsaturated margarine	32.6	10.	corn oil	17.2

smokers should ensure their diet contains plenty of vitamin E, as should the elderly in whom increased susceptibility to illness may be related to deficiency.

When obtained from food, vitamin E has no toxic effects. However, taking high-dose vitamin E supplements may cause breast soreness, muscle weakness, psychological and gastro-intestinal disturbance, and thyroid dysfunction.

VITAMIN K

There are two types of Vitamin K: phylloquinone (K1) is produced by plants involved in photosynthesis (those with green leaves); and menaquinone (K2) is produced by bacteria involved in fermentation (in foods such as cheese and tempeh). Intestinal bacteria also produce vitamin K, especially if we eat a high-fiber diet. Vitamin K is stored in the liver, and recycled many times before being broken down and excreted.

Vitamin K plays a vital role in normal blood clotting and bone health. It may help prevent osteoporosis and protect soft tissues from abnormal calcification. Deficiency is rare, but digestive diseases, such as celiac disease, pancreatitis, cystic fibrosis, and chronic liver disease, may cause deficiency since vitamin K depends on normal fat digestion for its own absorption. Symptoms of deficiency include easy bruising and bleeding, and bone fractures are also common in osteoporosis.

Hemorrhagic disease of the newborn (HDN) affects a small number of babies and was shown in the 1940s to be caused by vitamin K deficiency. Newborns used to be given protective vitamin K injections, but nowadays vitamin K is given to the mother before the birth, and to the baby by mouth once it is born. Natural vitamin K is non-toxic, even in large amounts.

Vitamin K TOP 10 (micrograms per 100 grams of food)

FDA guide to adequate intake = 120 µg/day for men; 90 µg/day for women. Toxicity level = none

1.	curly kale	623	6.	broccoli	185
2.	parsley	548	7.	brussels sprouts	153
3.	spinach	394	8.	lettuce	129
4.	watercress	315	9.	olive oil	57
5.	cabbage	242	10.	asparagus	52

Water-soluble vitamins

VITAMIN C

In the 18th century, scurvy was much feared by seafarers. The first signs were bleeding gums, leg pains, slow healing wounds, and general weakness, followed by hemorrhages under the skin, swellings, ulcers, and death. In 1772 James Lind (a Scottish physician) found that including citrus fruit in seamen's diets could cure scurvy in a week. Subsequent research showed that ascorbic acid, now known as vitamin C, was the key.

Vitamin C is an important antioxidant and plays a vital role in wound healing and iron absorption. It stimulates immune system cells to fight infections and helps lower blood cholesterol. It also reduces the toxic effects of radiation, and protects against serious diseases such as cancer and heart disease.

Unlike most animals, humans are unable to synthesize vitamin C, so we have to include it in our diet. Current recommended daily amounts are based on the amount necessary to protect against scurvy and promote wound healing, but many people could benefit from eating more. Animals that synthesize their own have much higher body levels of vitamin C than most humans, so it has been suggested that our vitamin C intake should be increased to produce similar levels. Cancer and rheumatoid arthritis sufferers have decreased amounts of vitamin C in their blood, as do smokers.

Today, scurvy appears only in cases of famine, severe malnutrition, malabsorption, and chronic alcoholism. However, people who take more than one gram of vitamin C supplements per day can develop signs of scurvy if they suddenly reduce their intake—even though their diet provides the recommended daily amount. Very high intakes of vitamin C can cause diarrhea and increase the risk of kidney stones.

Vitamin C TOP 10 (milligrams per 100 grams of food)

FDA recommended intake = 90 mg/day for men; 75 mg/day for women. Upper tolerable limit = 2 g/day

1.	guava	230	6.	brussels sprouts	115
2.	blackcurrants	200	7.	curly kale	110
3.	parsley	190	8.	broccoli	87
4.	beet greens	180	9.	watercress	62
5.	green, red, and chili peppers	120	10.	papaya (paw-paw)	60

VITAMIN B1 (THIAMIN)

Towards the end of the 19th century, an epidemic of beri-beri spread though Japan, China, and South-East Asia, causing serious problems for the colonial powers with their insatiable need for cheap labour. Mortality rates exceeded 50 per cent and, although it was noticed that the disease could be cured by supplementing the staple diet of rice with fish, vegetables, meat, and grains, poverty ensured that the epidemic continued. The cause of beri-beri only emerged when an "anti-beri-beri factor" (thiamin) was discovered in rice polishings—the parts of the rice grain removed during dehulling to produce polished white rice.

Vitamin B1 TOP 10 (milligrams per 100 grams of food)

THIAMIN

FDA recommended intake = 1.1–1.2 mg/day

Toxicity level = >3 g/day

1.	yeast extract	4.10	6.	pork	0.98
2.	wheat germ	2.01	7.	sesame seeds	0.94
3.	sunflower seeds	1.60	8.	oatmeal, wheat bran	0.90
4.	breakfast cereals		9.	peas	0.74
	(on average)	1.20	10.	brown rice	0.59
5.	peanuts	1.14			

The introduction of steam-powered mills and the production of polished rice on an industrial scale had robbed the rice grain of its nutrients, and the labourers who produced it of their health.

We need vitamin B1 (thiamin) to make use of the energy contained in carbohydrates, fats, and alcohol, so our daily requirement is closely linked to the amount of these foods in our diet. Foods containing carbohydrate and fat usually come ready-packed with thiamin, and a diet consisting of natural, unprocessed foods normally provides all that we need. In cereals and seeds, thiamin is found in the outer grain layers and is therefore often lost during milling and refining. To remedy this loss, many processed foods are fortified with vitamin B1.

Nowadays, vitamin B1 deficiency is associated with alcoholism, malnutrition, and chronic disease. In alcoholism, symptoms of B1 deficiency include confusion and loss of memory and balance. When deficiency becomes severe, beri-beri develops, causing muscle weakness, nerve problems, and eventually heart failure. Very high doses of thiamin (>3 g per day), and more moderate doses (>50 mg per day) taken over long periods, can cause toxicity symptoms, such as headaches, irritability, itching, eczema, fast pulse, sleepnessness, and weakness.

VITAMIN B2 (RIBOFLAVIN)

Vitamin B2 is used in the body to release energy from proteins, fats, and carbohydrates, and is found in small amounts in most foods. It is not well stored by the body, so the amount we need each day is related to how much food we eat and how many calories we spend. However much riboflavin we consume, the body only uses as much as it needs, excreting the rest in the urine. High doses of riboflavin supplements turn the urine bright yellow, but there are currently no other known side effects.

Vitamin B2 deficiency is uncommon, but those suffering from thyroid problems, diabetes, anorexia nervosa, severe malnutrition, and malabsorption syndromes may become deficient. Alcohol and some drugs (including chlorpromazine and barbiturates) can also reduce vitamin B2 levels in the body. The symptoms of deficiency include cracks at the corners of the mouth, a sore tongue and a rash around the nose. Riboflavin deficiency in infancy and childhood (ariboflavinosis) leads to retarded growth.

VITAMIN B3 (NIACIN)

Vitamin B3 is actually two different chemicals, nicotinic acid and nicotinamide. They form part of a system of co-enzymes responsible for the release of energy from food. Consequently, our daily requirement for niacin depends on the amount of food we eat and how much energy we use.

Niacin is found in most foods, and the essential amino acid tryptophan (present in many protein-rich foods) can also be converted into niacin in the body. This means that as long as we eat enough protein, we naturally meet our niacin requirements.

Vitamin B2 TOP 10 (milligrams per 100 grams of food)

RIBOFLAVIN
FDA recommended intake = 1.1–1.3 mg/day
Toxicity level = none known

1.	yeast extract	11.90	6.	wheat germ	0.72
2.	liver, heart, kidney		7.	venison, duck, goose	0.60
	(on average)	2.50	8.	tempeh	0.48
3.	breakfast cereals		9.	eggs, cheese	
	(on average)	1.20		(on average)	0.45
4.	crab	0.86	10.	oyster mushrooms	0.40
5.	almonds	0.75			

Vitamin B3 TOP 10 (milligrams per 100 grams of food)

NIACIN

FDA recommended intake = 14–16 mg/day

Upper tolerable limit = 35 mg/day

1.	yeast extract	71.0	6.	breakfast cereals		
2.	wheat bran	32.6		(on average)	15.0
3.	liver	19.4	7.	game	12.0
4.	peanuts	19.3	8.	sesame seeds	10.4
5.	paprika	18.4	9.	wheat germ	9.8
			10.	tempeh	4.7

Apart from helping to maintain energy levels, vitamin B3 is also involved in keeping skin and mucous membranes in good condition. Deficiency is rare, and is usually only seen in cases of severe malnourishment or in those subsisting on foods low in niacin and tryptophan, such as maize or millet. It also affects alcoholics and cancer sufferers, and can be caused by a genetic defect. Symptoms of niacin deficiency (also known as pellagra) include a red skin rash, sore tongue, constipation or diarrhea, weakness, insomnia, dementia, and mental disturbance.

While pellagra responds rapidly to treatment with niacin, there is no evidence that increased intake of the vitamin is of any benefit to people without the disease. High doses can cause low blood pressure, flushing, and excess stomach acid. Very high doses may also cause liver damage.

VITAMIN B5 (PANTOTHENATE)

Pantothenic means "that which is everywhere," and pantothenate, or pantothenic acid, is indeed present in almost all living tissues. It is found in most natural foods, and is produced by bacteria in the intestine. This vitamin enables the body to utilize the energy contained in fats, carbohydrates, protein, and alcohol. It aids antibody production, protects against allergy

Vitamin B5 TOP 10 (milligrams per 100 grams of food)

PANTOTHENATE
FDA recommended intake = 5 mg/day
Toxicity level = none

1.	fava beans	3.8	6.	wheat bran,	
2.	variety meats	3.8		wheat germ	2.2
3.	breakfast cereals		7.	sesame seeds	2.1
	(on average)	3.8	8.	mushrooms	2.0
4.	peanuts	2.7	9.	eggs	1.8
5.	cod roe	2.6	10.	trout	1.6

and hypertension, and maintains nervous system health. Vitamin B5 is also involved in the conversion of cholesterol into steroid hormones and in the detoxification of drugs. It is closely associated with the adrenal glands and with our ability to respond to stress, so it is also called "the stress vitamin."

Interestingly, research has shown that the aging process may be linked to the stress response, and that older people have lower blood levels of pantothenate than younger people.

Vitamin B5 deficiency is unlikely in people who eat a diet consisting mainly of fresh foods, but in affluent societies (where many people exist on refined, canned or frozen foods, white bread, and ready-made processed meals) sub-clinical pantothenate deficiency is becoming more common. Symptoms include weakness, insomnia, cramps and an increased tendency to allergy. Severe deficiency is very rare and causes pins and needles, a sensation of burning in the feet, low blood pressure, and inability of the adrenal glands to respond to stress.

VITAMIN B6 (PYRIDOXINE)

Vitamin B6 was first discovered in 1934. The more protein we eat, the more vitamin B6 we need because it is involved in protein metabolism and is necessary for the conversion of tryptophan into niacin. Vitamin B6 also facilitates hemoglobin production and protects against high blood pressure and allergy. It supports the nervous and immune systems, and is used to treat nausea in early pregnancy and during radiotherapy treatment.

Vitamin B6 deficiency is uncommon, but the likelihood increases with age. It is associated with alcoholism, chronic liver and kidney disease, intestinal malabsorption disorders, and

Vitamin B6 TOP 10 (milligrams per 100 grams of food)

PYRIDOXINE

WHO recommended intake = 1.3 mg/day (1.5–1.7 mg/day for over-50s). Toxicity level = individual tolerance varies (doses as low as 50 mg taken over long periods can cause neurological problems)

1.	wheat germ	3.30	6.	sesame seeds	0.76
2.	tempeh	1.86	7.	salmon	0.75
3.	muesli	1.60	8.	walnuts	0.67
4.	yeast extract	1.60	9.	venison	0.65
5.	wheat bran	1.38	10.	turkey	0.61

certain genetic disorders. It may also be linked to epilepsy, anemia, and carpal tunnel syndrome, and can be caused by the drugs used in the treatment of tuberculosis, rheumatoid arthritis, and Parkinson's disease. Mild deficiency in otherwise healthy people may diminish the immune response and increase the risk of atherosclerosis and hormone-dependent cancers.

Vitamin B6 is closely involved in hormone metabolism and the menstrual cycle. Sub-clinical deficiency is relatively common in women during childbearing years, especially those who have

---

Vitamin B12 TOP 10 (micrograms per 100 grams of food)

COBALAMIN
FDA recommended intake = 2.4 µg/day
Toxicity level = none

1.	liver, kidney	58.0	6.	prawns	8.0
2.	cockles, mussels	35.0	7.	salmon, trout,	
3.	nori seaweed (dried)	27.5		mackerel	5.0
4.	yeast extract,		8.	duck, rabbit, beef,	
	vegetable stock	13.3		lamb, turkey, goose	2.5
5.	kippers, sardines,		9.	eggs	2.5
	anchovies, cod roe	11.0	10.	cheese	2.0

Breakfast cereals and vegetable margarines are often fortified with B12.

had several pregnancies or who use oral contraceptives or HRT. Pre-menstrual mood swings, acne, and morning sickness—even pre-eclampsia and post-natal depression—may be related to vitamin B6 deficiency. Other symptoms include a skin rash around the eyes, nose, and mouth, cracks in the corners of the mouth and the lips, a sore tongue, migraine, depression, irritability, tiredness, and disturbed sensation in hands and feet.

Taking regular high doses of vitamin B6 over a long period can cause toxicity accompanied by loss of sensation in the hands and feet (which returns once intake is reduced).

VITAMIN B12 (COBALAMIN)

Vitamin B12 is produced entirely by micro-organisms living in the soil and in the intestines. It is used in DNA synthesis and is essential for all body cells, particularly blood and nerve cells. Rapidly dividing cells in the bone marrow need vitamin B12 and folic acid to produce red and white blood cells.

Vitamin B12 deficiency is rare because only tiny amounts are needed, and liver stores normally last four years. Malabsorption syndromes, intestinal parasites, alcoholism, and cancer are the most likely causes of deficiency. Smoking and

Folate TOP 10 (micrograms per 100 grams of food)

FDA recommended intake = 400 µg/day

Toxicity level = none (see opposite)

1.	yeast extract	2620		broccoli	195
2.	chicken liver	1350	8.	chick peas, mung and	
3.	blackeye beans	630		red kidney beans	180
4.	soy flour, soy beans	345	9.	asparagus, parsley,	
5.	wheat bran	260		swiss chard,	
6.	beef and lamb liver	250		savoy cabbage	170
7.	purple-sprouting		10.	beet	150

taking antibiotics also increase need, and strict vegetarians should include non-animal sources of B12 in their diet. Symptoms of deficiency include a sore tongue, diarrhea, and general weakness, progressing to numbness and tingling in fingers and toes, loss of balance, nerve pains and weakness in arms and legs caused by damage to the spinal cord and brain. Pernicious anemia is a rare form of vitamin B12 deficiency caused by a lack of "intrinsic factor"—a secretion in the stomach. Without intrinsic factor, B12 cannot be absorbed.

Vitamin B12 is non-toxic, even in large doses. People suffering from malabsorption syndromes (including pernicious anemia) usually need vitamin B12 injections.

FOLATE

Folate, or folic acid, is used by the body to produce amino acids and DNA. Together with vitamin B12, it supports rapidly dividing cells and is vitally important during pregnancy for the development of the baby's nervous system. Low folate in the diet has also been linked to heart disease.

Folate deficiency has three main causes: malnourishment, particularly among the elderly, the poor and alcoholics, but also increasingly in people whose diet consists mainly of fast foods; malabsorption, caused by gastro-intestinal disease and some drugs (particularly anti-epileptic medication); and increased need (owing to pregnancy, blood disorders, cancer, AIDS, and serious infection). The symptoms of deficiency include anemia, weakness, and depression. High folate intakes (usually from supplements) are not toxic, but can lead to reduced zinc absorption.

BIOTIN

Biotin is important for healthy skin, hair, sweat glands, nerves, and bone marrow. It also encourages the appetite and aids fat metabolism. It is found in most foods and is manufactured by gut bacteria. Like the other B-group vitamins, it plays a role in the conversion of calories into energy.

Biotin deficiency is rare, but can be caused by poor nutrition. Symptoms include dry skin, hair loss, fatigue, nausea, and lack of appetite. Severe deficiency causes muscle pains, pins and needles, anemia, and raised blood cholesterol. Biotin can be used to treat scalp conditions (such as hair loss and dandruff), skin problems (such as dry skin), and brittle nails.

Biotin TOP 10 (micrograms per 100 grams of food)

FDA recommended intake = 30 µg/day

Toxicity level = none

1.	chicken liver	216	6.	wheat bran	45
2.	peanuts	110	7.	wheat germ	25
3.	hazelnuts, almonds,		8.	eggs	20
	soy beans	65	9.	oatmeal, oatcakes	17
4.	tempeh	53	10.	mushrooms	15
5.	plaice	47			

VITAMIN TABLES

These tables give the calorie and vitamin contents of a wide selection of foods. The vitamins are divided into fat-soluble (vitamins A, D, and E) and water-soluble (vitamin C and the B-group—thiamin, riboflavin, niacin, pantothenate, pyridoxine, cobalamin, folate, and biotin). The calorie and vitamin contents of each food are given "per average portion" rather than by weight. This allows you to work out the calorie and vitamin content of your diet without using weights or measures.

To find out how rich a food is in a particular vitamin, compare the amount contained in a single portion ("n" is given where the figure for a particular food is not known; "tr" denotes trace) with the Quality Calorie Target (QCT) for that nutrient, given at the top of the relevant column. This will enable you to assess your daily intake of vitamins, and help you to choose particular foods to boost your intake of certain vitamins. The figures in bold denote the foods with the highest scores for each nutrient in each food category.

FRUIT

FOOD	AVERAGE PORTION SIZE	TOTAL CALORIES	FAT-SOLUBLE VITAMINS			
			A		D	
(where appropriate, numbers in brackets represent number of fruit in average portion)	oz per portion	kcals per portion	either Retinol (µg/portion) (QCT: 700µg/day)	or Carotene (µg/portion) (QCT: 4800µg/day)	Cholecalciferol (µg/portion) (QCT: 5µg/day*)	(* see pages 98–9)
Fresh fruit						
Apple (1)	3 ½	47	0	18	0	
Apricot (2)	4 ½	40	0	2,061	0	
Date (4)	3 ½	124	0	18	0	
Fig (2)	4	47	0	165	0	
Grapes (bunch)	3 ½	60	41	17	0	
Kiwi fruit (2)	4	59	0	44	0	
Melon (all types) (1 slice)	6 ½	43	0	1,800	0	
Peach/nectarine (1)	5	55	0	87	0	
Pear (1)	6	68	0	31	0	
Persimmon (1)	4	80	0	1,045	0	
Plum/greengage (2)	3 ½	39	0	195	0	
Rhubarb	3 ½	7	0	60	0	
Tropical fruit						
Banana (1)	3 ½	95	0	21	0	
Guava (1)	5	36	0	609	0	
Lychee (5)	2 ½	44	0	0	0	
Mango (½)	6 ½	103	0	**3,240**	0	
Papaya/paw-paw (¼)	5	50	0	1,134	0	
Passionfruit (5)	2 ½	27	0	563	0	
Pineapple (2 slices)	5 ½	66	0	29	0	
Pomegranate (1)	3 ½	51	0	33	0	
Citrus fruit						
Clementine/satsuma/tangerine (2)	4	43	0	108	0	
Grapefruit/pomelo (1)	6 ½	54	0	594	0	
Lemon/lime (1)	3 ½	12	0	tr	0	
Orange (1)	5 ½	59	0	45	0	
Berries						
Blackberries (20)	3 ½	25	0	80	0	
Blackcurrants	3 ½	28	0	100	0	

continues

	WATER-SOLUBLE VITAMINS									
E	**THE B-GROUP**									**C**
Tocopherol (mg/portion) (QCI: 15mg/day)	Thiamin B1 (mg/portion) (QCI: 1.1mg/day)	Riboflavin B2 (mg/portion) (QCI: 1.2mg/day)	Niacin B3 (mg/portion) (QCI: 15mg/day)	Pantothenate B5 (mg/portion) (QCI: 5mg/day)	Pyridoxine B6 (mg/portion) (QCI: 1.3mg/day)	Cobalamin B12 (µg/portion) (QCI: 2.4µg/day)	Folate (µg/portion) (QCI: 400µg/day)	Biotin (µg/portion) (QCI: 30µg/day)	Ascorbic acid (mg/portion) (QCI: 75mg/day)
0.6	tr	tr	0.2	tr	0.1	0	1	1	12
n	0.1	0.1	0.8	0.3	0.1	0	7	n	8
n	0.1	0.1	1.4	0.2	0.1	0	25	n	14
n	tr	tr	0.7	0.2	0.1	0	n	n	2
tr	0.1	tr	0.2	0.1	0.1	0	2	0	3
n	tr	tr	0.7	0.2	0.2	0	n	n	71
0.2	0.1	tr	0.7	0.3	0.2	0	5	n	31
tr	0.1	0.1	1.4	0.2	**0.5**	0	5	0	53
0.9	tr	0.1	0.3	0.1	tr	0	3	0	10
n	tr	0.1	0.3	n	n	0	8	n	21
0.7	0.1	tr	1.0	0.2	0.1	0	3	tr	5
0.2	tr	tr	0.4	0.1	n	0	7	n	6
0.3	tr	0.1	0.9	0.4	0.3	0	14	**3**	11
0.4	0.1	0.1	1.5	0.2	0.2	0	n	n	**322**
n	tr	0.1	0.5	n	n	0	n	n	34
1.9	0.1	0.1	3.2	0.3	0.2	0	n	n	67
n	tr	0.1	0.6	0.3	tr	0	1	n	84
n	tr	0.1	1.4	n	n	0	n	n	17
0.2	0.1	0.1	0.6	0.3	0.1	0	8	0	19
n	0.1	tr	0.5	0.6	tr	0	n	n	13
n	0.1	0.1	0.5	0.2	0.1	0	40	n	44
0.3	0.1	0.1	0.7	0.5	0.1	0	47	2	73
n	tr	tr	0.3	0.2	0.1	0	10	n	50
0.4	**0.2**	0.1	0.8	0.6	0.2	0	**50**	2	86
2.4	tr	0.1	0.6	0.3	0.1	0	34	0	15
1.0	tr	0.1	0.4	0.4	0.1	0	n	2	200

FRUIT

FOOD	AVERAGE PORTION SIZE	TOTAL CALORIES	FAT-SOLUBLE VITAMINS		
			A		D
(where appropriate, numbers in brackets represent number of fruit in average portion)	oz per portion	kcals per portion	either Retinol (μg/portion) (QCT: 700μg/day)	or Carotene (μg/portion) (QCT: 4800μg/day)	Cholecalciferol (μg/portion) (QCT: 5μg/day*)	(*see pages 98–9)
Blueberries (bilberries)	3 ½	30	0	30	0
Cherries (10)	3 ½	48	0	25	0
Cranberries	3 ½	15	0	22	0
Elderberries	3 ½	35	0	360	0
Gooseberries	3 ½	40	0	110	0
Raspberries (25)	3 ½	25	0	tr	0
Redcurrants	3 ½	21	0	25	0
Strawberries (10)	4	32	0	tr	0
Dried fruit					
Apricot (10)	3 ½	132	0	645	0
Date (6)	3 ½	203	0	40	0
Fig (5)	3 ½	227	0	64	0
Pear (10 slices)	3 ½	207	0	91	0
Pineapple (6 slices)	3 ½	276	0	120	0
Prune (10)	3 ½	160	0	155	0
Raisins (3 tbs)	3 ½	163	0	tr	0

| | | WATER-SOLUBLE VITAMINS | | | | | | | | |
| E | | | | | THE B-GROUP | | | | | C |
Tocopherol (mg/portion) (QCI: 15mg/day)	Thiamin B1 (mg/portion) (QCI: 1.1mg/day)	Riboflavin B2 (mg/portion) (QCI: 1.2mg/day)	Niacin B3 (mg/portion) (QCI: 15mg/day)	Pantothenate B5 (mg/portion) (QCI: 5mg/day)	Pyridoxine B6 (mg/portion) (QCI: 1.3mg/day)	Cobalamin B12 (µg/portion) (QCI: 2.4µg/day)	Folate (µg/portion) (QCI: 400µg/day)	Biotin (µg/portion) (QCI: 30µg/day)	Ascorbic acid (mg/portion) (QCI: 75mg/day)
n	tr	tr	0.5	0.3	0.1	0	6	1	17
0.1	tr	tr	0.3	0.3	0.1	0	5	0	11
n	tr	tr	0.2	0.2	0.1	0	2	n	13
n	0.1	0.1	1.1	0.2	0.2	0	17	2	27
0.4	tr	tr	0.5	0.3	tr	0	8	1	14
0.5	tr	0.1	0.8	0.2	0.1	0	33	2	32
0.1	tr	0.1	0.3	0.1	0.1	0	n	3	40
0.2	tr	tr	0.8	0.4	0.1	0	24	1	92
n	tr	0.2	3.6	0.7	0.2	0	14	n	tr
n	0.1	0.1	3.3	0.8	0.2	0	13	n	tr
n	0.1	0.1	1.3	0.5	0.3	0	9	n	1
tr	n	n	n	n	n	0	tr	n	tr
0.7	n	n	n	n	n	0	tr	n	tr
n	0.1	0.2	2.0	0.5	0.2	0	4	tr	tr
n	0.1	0.1	0.8	0.2	0.3	0	19	3	1

NUTS AND SEEDS

FOOD	AVERAGE PORTION SIZE	TOTAL CALORIES	FAT-SOLUBLE VITAMINS			
				A	D	
	oz per portion	kcals per portion	either Retinol (µg/portion) (QCT: 700µg/day)	or Carotene (µg/portion) (QCT: 4800µg/day)	Cholecalciferol (µg/portion) (QCT: 5µg/day*)	(*see pages 98–9)
Almonds	1 ¾	306	0	0	0	
Brazil nuts	1 ¾	341	0	0	0	
Cashew nuts	1 ¾	287	0	0	0	
Chestnuts, dried	1 ¾	160	0	0	0	
Coconut, fresh	3 ½	351	0	0	0	
Coconut, desiccated	1 ¾	302	0	0	0	
Hazelnuts	1 ¾	325	0	0	0	
Macadamia nuts (salted)	1 ¾	374	0	0	0	
Melon seeds	1 ¾	292	0	0	0	
Peanuts	1 ¾	282	0	0	0	
Peanut butter	¾	125	0	0	0	
Pecan nuts	1 ¾	345	0	25	0	
Pine nuts	1 ¾	344	0	5	0	
Pistachio nuts (salted)	1 ¾	301	0	65	0	
Pumpkin seeds	1 ¾	285	0	115	0	
Sesame seeds	1 ¾	299	0	3	0	
Sesame spread (tahini)	1 ¾	304	0	0	0	
Sunflower seeds	1 ¾	291	0	7	0	
Walnuts	1 ¾	344	0	0	0	

| | | | | | WATER-SOLUBLE VITAMINS | | | | |
| E | | | | | | | THE B-GROUP | | C |
Tocopherol (mg/portion) (QCT: 15mg/day)	Thiamin B1 (mg/portion) (QCT: 1.1mg/day)	Riboflavin B2 (mg/portion) (QCT: 1.2mg/day)	Niacin B3 (mg/portion) (QCT: 15mg/day)	Pantothenate B5 (mg/portion) (QCT: 5mg/day)	Pyridoxine B6 (mg/portion) (QCT: 1.3mg/day)	Cobalamin B12 (μg/portion) (QCT: 2.4μg/day)	Folate (μg/portion) (QCT: 400μg/day)	Biotin (μg/portion) (QCT: 30μg/day)	Ascorbic acid (mg/portion) (QCT: 75mg/day)
12.0	0.1	**0.4**	3.3	0.2	0.1	0	24	32	0
3.6	0.3	0	1.7	0.2	0.2	0	24	6	0
0.4	0.3	0.1	2.9	0.5	0.2	0	34	6	0
1.2	0.1	0	0.9	0.5	0.3	0	n	1	0
0.7	0	0	1.1	0.3	0.1	0	26	n	**3**
0.6	0	0	1.0	0.3	0	0	5	n	0
12.5	0.2	0.1	2.6	0.8	0.3	0	36	**38**	0
0.7	0.1	0	1.7	0.3	0.1	0	n	3	0
n	0.1	0.1	5.9	n	n	0	29	n	0
5.0	0.6	0.1	**9.7**	**1.3**	0.3	0	**55**	36	0
1.0	0	0	3.5	0.3	0.1	0	11	19	0
2.2	0.4	0.1	2.8	0.9	0.1	0	20	n	0
6.8	0.4	0.1	3.5	n	n	0	n	n	0
2.1	0.4	0.1	2.8	n	n	0	29	n	0
n	0.1	0.2	4.4	n	n	0	n	n	0
1.3	0.5	0.1	5.2	1.1	**0.4**	0	49	6	0
1.3	0.5	0.1	4.6	1.1	**0.4**	0	50	6	0
18.9	**0.8**	0.1	4.6	n	n	0	n	n	0
1.9	0.2	0.1	2.0	0.8	0.3	0	33	10	0

VEGETABLES AND PULSES

FOOD	AVERAGE PORTION SIZE oz per portion	TOTAL CALORIES kcals per portion	FAT-SOLUBLE VITAMINS			
				A	D	
			either Retinol (µg/portion) (QCT: 700µg/day)	or Carotene (µg/portion) (QCT: 4800µg/day)	Cholecalciferol (µg/portion) (QCT: 5µg/day*)	(*see pages 98–9)
Root vegetables						
Beet	3 ½	36	0	27	0	
Carrot	3 ½	35	0	**8,115**	0	
Celeriac	3 ½	18	0	26	0	
Parsnip	3 ½	64	0	30	0	
Potato, baked	6 ½	245	0	tr	0	
Potato, boiled in salted water	6 ½	130	0	tr	0	
Potato, mashed	6 ½	187	74	68	0.7	
Potato, fries (all types, average)	6 ½	398	0	tr	0	
Rutabaga	3 ½	24	0	350	0	
Sweet potato, baked	4 ½	150	0	6,682	0	
Beans, peas, and lentils						
Aduki beans, cooked	3 ½	123	0	6	0	
Baked beans, in tomato sauce	4 ½	105	0	91	0	
Bean sprouts, fresh	2	19	0	24	0	
Blackeye/pigeon/mung beans (av.)	3 ½	99	0	12	0	
Chick peas, cooked	3 ½	121	0	23	0	
Fava beans, fresh	4	71	0	204	0	
Green beans (haricots verts), fresh	3 ½	24	0	330	0	
Haricot beans, dried, cooked	3 ½	95	0	tr	0	
Lentils, cooked (all types, av.)	3 ½	105	0	20	0	
Lima beans, cooked	3 ½	103	0	tr	0	
Peas, fresh	3 ½	83	0	300	0	
Pinto beans, cooked	3 ½	137	0	tr	0	
Red kidney beans, cooked	3 ½	103	0	tr	0	
String beans, yard-long, fresh	3 ½	22	0	145	0	
Soy beans, black, cooked	3 ½	141	0	tr	0	
Tempeh (fermented soybean)	3 ½	166	0	tr	0	
Tofu (soybean curd)	3 ½	73	0	tr	0	

continues

	WATER-SOLUBLE VITAMINS									
E	**THE B-GROUP**									**C**
Tocopherol (mg/portion) (QCI: 15mg/day)	Thiamin B1 (mg/portion) (QCI: 1.1mg/day)	Riboflavin B2 (mg/portion) (QCI: 1.2mg/day)	Niacin B3 (mg/portion) (QCI: 15mg/day)	Pantothenate B5 (mg/portion) (QCI: 5mg/day)	Pyridoxine B6 (mg/portion) (QCI: 1.3mg/day)	Cobalamin B12 (µg/portion) (QCI: 2.4µg/day)	Folate (µg/portion) (QCI: 400µg/day)	Biotin (µg/portion) (QCI: 30µg/day)	Ascorbic acid (mg/portion) (QCI: 75mg/day)
tr	tr	tr	0.4	0.1	tr	0	150	tr	5
0.6	0.1	tr	0.3	0.3	0.1	0	12	1	6
n	0.2	tr	0.4	n	0.1	0	51	n	14
1.0	0.2	tr	1.5	0.5	0.1	0	87	0	17
0.2	**0.7**	tr	3.6	0.8	1.0	0	79	1	25
0.1	0.3	tr	1.6	0.7	0.6	0	47	1	11
0.8	0.3	tr	1.6	0.6	0.5	tr	43	1	9
1.3	0.2	0.1	2.9	n	0.6	0	38	n	16
tr	0.2	tr	1.3	0.1	0.2	0	31	0	31
7.7	0.1	tr	1.0	0.8	0.1	0	n	0	30
n	0.1	0.1	2.4	n	n	0	n	n	tr
0.5	0.1	0.1	1.7	0.2	0.2	0	43	3	tr
0.1	0.1	tr	0.6	0.2	0.1	0	37	n	4
0.4	0.2	0.1	1.9	0.4	0.1	0	93	7	tr
1.1	0.1	0.1	1.8	0.3	0.1	0	54	n	tr
0.6	tr	tr	**4.9**	**5.9**	0.1	0	174	3	38
0.2	0.1	0.1	1.4	0.1	0.1	0	80	1	12
0.1	0.1	tr	1.7	0.2	0.1	0	n	n	tr
n	0.1	0.1	1.8	0.3	0.3	0	30	n	tr
0.4	0.2	0.1	1.5	0.4	0.2	0	n	n	tr
0.2	**0.7**	tr	3.6	0.2	0.1	0	62	1	24
n	0.2	0.1	1.7	0.3	0.2	0	145	n	2
0.2	0.2	0.1	1.9	0.2	0.1	0	42	n	1
0.2	0.1	tr	0.8	0.1	0.1	0	60	1	18
1.1	0.1	0.1	2.7	0.2	0.2	0	54	25	tr
1.0	0.1	tr	1.4	1.1	**1.9**	**1.0**	76	**53**	0
1.0	0.1	tr	1.4	4.9	0.1	0	15	n	0

VEGETABLES AND PULSES

FOOD	AVERAGE PORTION SIZE	TOTAL CALORIES	FAT-SOLUBLE VITAMINS		D	
			A			
(where appropriate, numbers in brackets represent number of vegetables in average portion)	oz per portion	kcals per portion	either Retinol (µg/portion) (QCT: 700µg/day)	or Carotene (µg/portion) (QCT: 4800µg/day)	Cholecalciferol (µg/portion) (QCT: 5µg/day*)	(*see pages 98–9)
Miscellaneous vegetables						
Artichoke hearts (2)	3 ½	18	0	90	0	
Asparagus (5 spears)	4 ½	31	0	394	0	
Avocado (1)	5	276	0	23	0	
Beet greens	3 ½	33	0	2,630	0	
Broccoli, green/purple	3 ½	34	0	630	0	
Brussels sprouts (9)	3 ½	42	0	215	0	
Cabbage (all types, average)	3 ½	26	0	385	0	
Cauliflower	3 ½	34	0	tr	0	
Celery (3 sticks)	3 ½	7	0	50	0	
Chicory	3 ½	13	0	440	0	
Cucumber (2 in chunk)	4	12	0	192	0	
Curly kale	3 ½	33	0	3,145	0	
Eggplant (½)	4 ½	20	0	91	0	
Fennel	3 ½	12	0	140	0	
Lettuce (all types, average)	2 ¾	10	0	728	0	
Mushrooms, common	3 ¼	13	0	0	0	
Mushrooms, shiitake	1 ¾	28	0	0	0	
Okra (gumbo)	3 ½	31	0	515	0	
Olive (10)	1	31	0	tr	0	
Onion/leek (all types, average)	3 ½	28	0	350	0	
Pepper, green/red (½)**	2 ¾	19	0	212	0	
Pumpkin	6 ½	23	0	1,719	0	
Seaweed, dried (all types, av.)***	½	8	0	527	0	
Spinach	3 ½	25	0	3,535	0	
Sweetcorn	3 ½	93	0	97	0	
Swiss chard	3 ½	19	0	4,625	0	
Tomato (1)	3	14	0	544	0	
Watercress	3	18	0	2,016	0	
Zucchini	3 ½	18	0	610	0	

**the carotene amount given is for green pepper – red pepper contains 3,070µg
***nori contains the highest level of vitamin B12

| E | WATER-SOLUBLE VITAMINS | | | | | | | | C |
| | | | | | THE B-GROUP | | | | |
Tocopherol (mg/portion) (QCI: 15mg/day)	Thiamin B1 (mg/portion) (QCI: 1.1mg/day)	Riboflavin B2 (mg/portion) (QCI: 1.2mg/day)	Niacin B3 (mg/portion) (QCI: 15mg/day)	Pantothenate B5 (mg/portion) (QCI: 5mg/day)	Pyridoxine B6 (mg/portion) (QCI: 1.3mg/day)	Cobalamin B12 (µg/portion) (QCI: 2.4µg/day)	Folate (µg/portion) (QCI: 400µg/day)	Biotin (µg/portion) (QCI: 30µg/day)	Ascorbic acid (mg/portion) (QCI: 75mg/day)
0.2	0.1	0.1	1.8	0.3	tr	0	68	4	2
1.5	0.2	0.1	1.9	0.2	0.1	0	**219**	1	15
4.6	0.1	**0.3**	2.0	1.6	0.5	0	16	5	9
n	0.1	0.1	2.0	0.4	0.2	0	92	0	**180**
1.3	0.1	0.1	1.3	1.0	0.2	0	143	1	100
1.0	0.2	0.1	0.9	1.0	0.4	0	135	0	115
0.5	0.2	tr	0.8	0.2	0.2	0	75	tr	49
0.2	0.2	0.1	1.5	0.6	0.3	0	66	2	43
0.2	0.1	tr	0.4	0.4	tr	0	16	tr	8
n	0.1	0.1	0.6	0.9	tr	0	140	1	12
0.1	tr	tr	0.4	0.4	tr	0	11	1	2
1.7	0.1	0.1	1.7	0.1	0.3	0	120	1	110
tr	tr	tr	0.4	0.1	0.1	0	23	n	5
n	0.1	tr	0.6	n	0.1	0	42	n	5
0.5	0.1	tr	0.5	0.1	0.1	0	46	1	6
0.1	0.1	**0.3**	3.5	2.0	0.2	0	44	12	1
n	tr	0.1	0.8	n	n	n	n	n	tr
n	0.2	0.1	1.4	0.3	0.2	0	88	n	21
0.6	tr	tr	tr	tr	tr	0	tr	tr	0
0.6	0.2	0.1	0.8	0.1	0.4	0	40	1	11
0.6	0.0	tr	0.6	0.1	0.3	0	22	n	104
1.9	0.3	tr	0.4	0.7	tr	0	18	1	25
n	tr	0.1	0.4	n	tr	**1.0**	n	n	1
1.7	0.1	0.1	1.9	0.3	0.2	0	150	tr	26
0.7	0.2	0.1	2.3	0.7	0.2	0	41	n	8
n	tr	0.1	0.7	0.2	n	0	165	n	30
1.0	0.1	tr	0.9	0.2	0.1	0	14	1	14
1.2	0.1	tr	0.6	0.1	0.2	0	n	0	50
n	0.1	tr	0.6	0.1	0.2	0	52	n	21

VEGETABLE DISHES

FOOD	AVERAGE PORTION SIZE	TOTAL CALORIES	FAT-SOLUBLE VITAMINS			
				A	D	
(where appropriate, numbers in brackets represent number of items in average portion)	oz per portion	kcals per portion	either Retinol (µg/portion) (QCT: 700µg/day)	or Carotene (µg/portion) (QCT: 4800µg/day)	Cholecalciferol (µg/portion) (QCT: 5µg/day*)	(*see pages 98–9)
Bakes and flans						
Cannelloni	7	290	112	986	n	
Casserole, bean and vegetable	9	115	0	2,928	0	
Cauliflower cheese	7	210	140	145	0.5	
Cottage pie, vegetable	10	339	87	1,755	tr	
Flan, vegetable	4	253	92	2,606	0.7	
Lasagne, vegetable	16	527	n	n	n	
Moussaka, vegetable	12	480	n	n	n	
Nut roast	5	528	0	26	0	
Pizza, cheese and tomato	10	711	177	369	**5.4**	
Burgers, cutlets, and pancakes						
Beanburger (no bun)	2 ½	152	0	143	0	
Dosa with vegetable filling (1)	7	307	0	530	0	
Falafel (3)	3 ½	179	0	230	0	
Nut cutlet (2)	4	347	0	624	0	
Onion bhaji/pakora (1)	1 ¾	156	0	55	0	
Pancake with vegetable filling (1)	7	298	132	300	1.4	
Quorn (myco-protein)	3 ½	86	0	0	0	
Samosa, vegetable (1)	3 ½	217	0	n	0	
Tempeh burger (1)	2	116	0	5	0	
Tofu burger (1)	2	71	0	396	tr	
Vegeburger (1)	2	147	n	tr	n	
Curries, stews, and rice dishes						
Bhaji, cauliflower	9	535	0	463	0	
Bhaji, mushroom	9	415	0	263	0	
Bhaji, potato	9	395	0	50	0	
Broccoli in cheese sauce	7	236	160	690	0.6	
Colcannon (fried)	7	248	0	822	0	
Curry, cauliflower and potato	9	148	0	245	0	
Curry, chick pea and spinach	9	498	0	2,438	0	

continues

| | WATER-SOLUBLE VITAMINS | | | | | | | | |
| E | | | | | THE B-GROUP | | | | C |
Tocopherol (mg/portion) (QCT: 15mg/day)	Thiamin B1 (mg/portion) (QCT: 1.1mg/day)	Riboflavin B2 (mg/portion) (QCT: 1.2mg/day)	Niacin B3 (mg/portion) (QCT: 15mg/day)	Pantothenate B5 (mg/portion) (QCT: 5mg/day)	Pyridoxine B6 (mg/portion) (QCT: 1.3mg/day)	Cobalamin B12 (µg/portion) (QCT: 2.4µg/day)	Folate (µg/portion) (QCT: 400µg/day)	Biotin (µg/portion) (QCT: 30µg/day)	Ascorbic acid (mg/portion) (QCT: 75mg/day)
0.5	0.2	0.3	2.8	0.3	0.1	0.8	8	1	6
1.6	0.3	0.2	3.8	0.5	0.4	0	44	1	14
2.5	0.3	0.3	4.5	1.1	0.5	0.8	63	5	38
2.3	0.3	tr	2.4	0.7	0.5	tr	30	2	12
3.1	0.1	0.1	2.2	n	0.1	0.4	23	n	10
n	1.1	1.3	14.0	n	2.0	n	27	n	n
n	0.2	2.5	7.0	n	0.6	tr	42	n	n
8.3	0.7	0.5	14.4	1.3	0.4	tr	72	35	0
7.6	0.5	0.4	12.3	0.6	0.1	3.0	21	12	3
0.2	0.2	0.1	0.2	0.1	0.1	0	17	14	3
4.0	0.2	0.1	3.9	0.5	0.4	0	33	2	6
3.2	0.1	0.1	1.7	0.5	0.2	0	26	n	8
2.3	0.2	0.1	0.2	0.1	n	0	0	0	0
2.2	0.1	0.1	1.3	0.4	0.1	0	20	0	0
1.2	0.2	0.2	3.4	0.9	0.2	0.6	22	7	6
0	3.7	0.2	0.3	0.1	tr	0	7	9	0
n	0.1	0.1	0.2	n	0.2	0	44	n	n
0.9	0.1	0.1	1.1	n	n	0	8	n	tr
1.1	0.1	tr	1.0	0.2	0.1	0	10	n	1
n	1.3	0.2	3.7	n	0.2	0	49	n	n
12.4	0.4	0.1	4.0	1.3	0.6	0	88	3	60
10.0	0.3	0.4	5.0	2.3	0.4	0	40	14	5
6.1	0.4	0.1	2.5	0.7	0.9	0	43	1	18
2.0	0.1	0.3	3.8	n	0.2	0.6	86	n	54
n	0.2	tr	1.4	0.5	0.3	0	24	0	1
1.7	0.4	0.1	3.5	1.1	0.7	0	75	3	2
10.4	0.2	0.2	3.8	0.9	0.3	0	83	n	5

VEGETABLE DISHES

FOOD	AVERAGE PORTION SIZE	TOTAL CALORIES	FAT-SOLUBLE VITAMINS		
			A		D
(where appropriate, numbers in brackets represent number of items in average portion)	oz per portion	kcals per portion	either Retinol (µg/portion) (QCT: 700µg/day)	or Carotene (µg/portion) (QCT: 4800µg/day)	Cholecalciferol (µg/portion) (QCT: 5µg/day*)	(*see pages 98–9)
Curry, red lentil and mung bean	9	285	0	190	0
Curry, red lentil and tomato	9	230	0	988	0
Curry, okra	9	273	0	1,225	0
Curry, mixed vegetable	9	123	0	2,313	0
Okra with tomato and onion	9	450	0	1,588	0
Ratatouille	9	205	0	463	0
Risotto (brown rice)	12	501	0	1,803	0
Side dishes, dips, spreads, and sauces					
Guacamole	3 ½	128	0	190	0
Houmous	2	112	0	n	0
Pesto sauce	1	129	38	163	0
Red cabbage, stewed with apple	3 ½	59	0	37	0
Tofu spread	1 ¾	104	0	135	0
Vegetable pâté	1 ¾	87	tr	n	tr
Vegetable stir-fry	3 ½	64	0	n	0
Vine leaves, stuffed with rice (3)	3 ½	262	0	420	0
Salads					
Coleslaw, with vinaigrette	3 ½	87	0	735	0
Salad, bean, with vinaigrette	3 ½	147	0	250	0
Salad, beet, with vinaigrette	3 ½	100	0	22	0
Salad, carrot, nut, with vinaigrette	3 ½	218	0	**5,165**	0
Salad, Greek	3 ½	130	30	260	0.1
Salad, green (no dressing)	3 ½	12	0	195	0
Salad, pasta, veg., w. mayonnaise	3 ½	127	7	1,365	tr
Salad, potato, with vinaigrette	3 ½	157	0	50	0
Salad, potato, with mayonnaise	3 ½	239	23	70	0.1
Salad, Waldorf	3 ½	193	15	34	0.1
Tabouleh/couscous salad	3 ½	119	0	260	0

E											WATER-SOLUBLE VITAMINS	C
										THE B-GROUP	
Tocopherol (mg/portion) (QCI: 15mg/day)	Thiamin B1 (mg/portion) (QCI: 1.1mg/day)	Riboflavin B2 (mg/portion) (QCI: 1.2mg/day)	Niacin B3 (mg/portion) (QCI: 15mg/day)	Pantothenate B5 (mg/portion) (QCI: 5mg/day)	Pyridoxine B6 (mg/portion) (QCI: 1.3mg/day)	Cobalamin B12 (µg/portion) (QCI: 2.4µg/day)	Folate (µg/portion) (QCI: 400µg/day)	Biotin (µg/portion) (QCI: 30µg/day)	Ascorbic acid (mg/portion) (QCI: 75mg/day)
3.9	0.2	0.1	2.8	0.6	0.2	0	20	n	tr
4.7	0.2	0.1	2.5	0.5	0.3	0	13	n	13
n	0.4	0.1	3.3	0.5	0.5	0	80	n	23
2.0	0.2	0.1	1.8	0.4	0.3	0	38	2	18
n	0.5	0.1	3.5	0.6	0.5	0	**105**	n	30
6.7	0.2	0.1	2.0	n	0.4	0	103	n	35
4.4	0.6	0.3	8.1	1.5	0.4	0	42	n	35
2.4	0.1	0.1	1.2	0.8	0.3	0	12	3	11
n	0.1	tr	1.3	n	n	0	n	n	1
0.9	tr	0.1	1.4	n	n	0.2	n	n	1
0.2	tr	tr	0.5	0.2	0.1	0	14	0	21
2.5	tr	tr	0.4	tr	tr	0	7	n	2
n	1.1	0.7	3.2	n	0.2	tr	55	n	tr
n	0.1	0.1	1.3	n	0.3	0	16	n	8
1.1	0.1	0.1	0.9	0.1	0.1	0	6	1	4
0.9	0.1	tr	0.5	0.2	0.1	0	24	tr	24
0.5	0.1	tr	1.3	0.1	0.1	0	44	n	6
tr	tr	tr	0.5	0.1	0.1	0	86	tr	5
3.0	0.1	tr	0.8	0.3	0.2	0	17	9	4
1.1	tr	tr	1.0	0.2	0.1	0.1	16	n	26
0.4	0.1	tr	0.3	0.2	0.1	0	29	n	36
2.0	tr	tr	0.9	n	0.1	tr	16	n	21
0.1	0.2	tr	0.7	0.3	0.3	0	23	tr	7
5.3	0.1	tr	0.8	n	0.2	0.1	21	n	6
3.8	0.1	tr	0.1	0.2	0.1	0.1	7	n	5
1.2	0.1	tr	0.4	n	n	0	17	n	13

MEAT AND MEAT DISHES

FOOD	AVERAGE PORTION SIZE	TOTAL CALORIES	FAT-SOLUBLE VITAMINS			
				A	D	
	oz per portion	kcals per portion	either Retinol (µg/portion) (QCT: 700µg/day)	or Carotene (µg/portion) (QCT: 4800µg/day)	Cholecalciferol (µg/portion) (QCT: 5µg/day*)	(*see pages 98–9)
Beef						
Ground	7	458	tr	tr	tr	
Roast	4	341	tr	tr	tr	
Steak	4	295	tr	tr	tr	
Veal cutlet	5	323	tr	tr	tr	
Lamb						
Chop	5 ½	443	tr	tr	tr	
Cutlet	3 ½	244	tr	tr	tr	
Roast	4	319	tr	tr	tr	
Pork						
Bacon	3 ½	477	tr	tr	tr	
Chop	4	395	tr	tr	tr	
Roast	4	343	tr	tr	tr	
Poultry and game						
Chicken, roast	4	259	tr	tr	tr	
Duck, roast	4	407	n	n	n	
Goose, roast	4	383	n	n	n	
Grouse, roast	4	208	n	n	n	
Pheasant, roast	4	256	n	n	n	
Rabbit, roast or stewed	4	230	n	n	n	
Squab, roast	4	276	n	n	n	
Turkey, roast	4	205	tr	tr	tr	
Venison, roast or stewed	4	238	n	n	n	
Variety meats						
Heart (all types, average)	3 ½	208	tr	tr	n	
Kidney (all types, average)	3 ½	160	123	n	n	
Liver (all types, average)	3 ½	213	**13,540**	340	0.6	
Oxtail	3 ½	243	tr	tr	tr	
Tripe	5	150	tr	tr	tr	

continues

Tocopherol (mg/portion) (QCI: 15mg/day)	Thiamin B1 (mg/portion) (QCI: 1.1mg/day)	Riboflavin B2 (mg/portion) (QCI: 1.2mg/day)	Niacin B3 (mg/portion) (QCI: 15mg/day)	Pantothenate B5 (mg/portion) (QCI: 5mg/day)	Pyridoxine B6 (mg/portion) (QCI: 1.3mg/day)	Cobalamin B12 (µg/portion) (QCI: 2.4µg/day)	Folate (µg/portion) (QCI: 400µg/day)	Biotin (µg/portion) (QCI: 30µg/day)	Ascorbic acid (mg/portion) (QCI: 75mg/day)
0.6	0.1	0.7	18.6	1.6	0.6	4.0	32	tr	0
0.4	0.1	0.3	11.8	0.8	0.3	2.0	17	tr	0
0.4	tr	0.4	13.4	1.0	0.4	2.0	19	tr	0
n	n	n	10.1	n	n	2.0	tr	tr	0
0.1	0.1	0.3	12.6	0.6	0.2	3.0	3	2	0
0.1	0.1	0.1	6.4	0.4	0.2	1.0	3	1	0
0.1	0.1	0.4	13.2	0.7	0.2	2.0	4	1	0
0.2	0.4	0.2	9.5	0.3	0.3	tr	1	2	0
tr	0.7	0.2	8.6	0.8	0.3	2.0	4	2	0
tr	**0.8**	0.3	12.0	1.2	0.4	1.0	tr	2	0
0.1	0.1	0.2	15.4	1.4	0.3	tr	12	4	0
tr	0.3	0.6	12.6	1.4	0.3	4.0	12	2	0
n	n	n	6.6	n	0.5	n	n	n	n
n	0.4	0.6	17.5	n	n	n	n	n	n
n	tr	0.2	14.5	n	n	n	n	n	0
0.2	0.1	0.3	16.3	1.0	0.6	14.0	5	1	0
tr	n	n	16.9	n	n	n	n	n	0
tr	0.1	0.3	16.7	1.0	0.4	2.0	18	2	0
n	0.3	n	7.8	n	n	n	n	n	n
0.4	0.5	0.9	10.5	2.5	0.3	10.0	3	3	7
0.3	0.4	1.9	10.8	3.1	0.3	33.0	50	31	10
0.3	0.3	**3.1**	16.8	7.5	0.6	**75.0**	**298**	**70**	17
0.3	tr	0.3	8.8	1.0	0.3	3.0	7	1	0
0.1	tr	0.1	4.8	0.3	tr	tr	2	3	5

MEAT AND MEAT DISHES

FOOD	AVERAGE PORTION SIZE	TOTAL CALORIES	FAT-SOLUBLE VITAMINS			
				A	D	
(where appropriate, numbers in brackets represent number of items in average portion)	oz per portion	kcals per portion	either Retinol (µg/portion) (QCI: 700µg/day)	or Carotene (µg/portion) (QCI: 4800µg/day)	Cholecalciferol (µg/portion) (QCI: 5µg/day*)	(*see pages 98–9)
Cold meats						
Corned beef	1	54	tr	tr	tr	
Ham	1	30	tr	tr	tr	
Processed meat	1	78	tr	tr	tr	
Tongue (pressed)	1	53	tr	tr	tr	
Burgers and sausages						
Beefburger, quarterpounder	2 ¾	211	tr	tr	tr	
Liver sausage (1)	1 ¾	155	4,150	tr	0.3	
Salami (2 slices)	1	167	tr	tr	tr	
Sausage (all types, average) (1)	1 ¾	157	tr	tr	tr	
Turkey burger/escalope	3 ¼	119	tr	tr	tr	
Meat dishes						
Black pudding	2 ½	229	tr	tr	tr	
Bolognese sauce	7 ¾	306	tr	4,268	tr	
Chicken chow mein	12	515	tr	385	n	
Cornish pasty	5 ½	515	tr	tr	tr	
Cottage pie	10	357	42	tr	0.4	
Haggis	3 ½	310	1,800	tr	0.1	
Hot pot	11 ½	376	tr	6,270	tr	
Irish stew	11 ½	409	tr	tr	tr	
Lamb curry	11 ½	528	tr	tr	tr	
Lasagne	12	669	175	1,817	1.4	
Moussaka	11 ½	644	99	215	0.2	
Pork pie	5	564	tr	tr	tr	
Samosa (lamb)	3 ½	578	15	37	0.7	
Sausage roll	2	287	75	tr	0.5	
Shish kebab (in pita with salad)	9 ½	419	tr	324	0.5	
Spring roll	3 ½	242	tr	175	n	
Steak and kidney pie	7	646	n	n	n	
Tandoori chicken	12	749	tr	735	0.7	

| | WATER-SOLUBLE VITAMINS | | | | | | | | |
| E | | | THE B-GROUP | | | | | | C |
Tocopherol (mg/portion) (QCI: 15mg/day)	Thiamin B1 (mg/portion) (QCI: 1.1mg/day)	Riboflavin B2 (mg/portion) (QCI: 1.2mg/day)	Niacin B3 (mg/portion) (QCI: 15mg/day)	Pantothenate B5 (mg/portion) (QCI: 5mg/day)	Pyridoxine B6 (mg/portion) (QCI: 1.3mg/day)	Cobalamin B12 (µg/portion) (QCI: 2.4µg/day)	Folate (µg/portion) (QCI: 400µg/day)	Biotin (µg/portion) (QCI: 30µg/day)	Ascorbic acid (mg/portion) (QCI: 75mg/day)
0.2	tr	0.1	2.3	0.1	tr	1.0	tr	1	0
tr	0.1	0.1	1.7	0.2	0.1	tr	tr	0	0
tr	tr	tr	1.1	0.1	tr	0	tr	tr	0
0.1	tr	0.1	1.6	0.1	tr	1.0	1	1	0
0.5	tr	0.2	6.4	0.4	0.2	2.0	12	2	0
0.1	0.1	0.8	3.8	0.8	0.1	4.0	10	4	tr
0.1	0.1	0.1	2.8	0.3	0.1	0	1	1	0
0.2	tr	0.1	2.7	0.3	0	1.0	tr	1	0
tr	0.1	0.1	14.0	0.6	0.3	1.0	12	1	0
0.2	0.1	0.1	2.9	0.5	tr	1.0	4	2	0
2.9	0.1	0.3	7.3	0.9	0.4	2.0	22	tr	11
3.4	0.2	0.1	10.9	1.6	0.3	tr	14	7	tr
2.0	0.2	0.1	5.1	0.9	0.2	2.0	5	2	0
0.8	0.1	0.4	9.6	0.9	0.5	3.0	21	tr	6
0.4	0.2	0.4	3.5	0.5	0.1	2.0	8	12	tr
0.7	0.2	0.3	12.5	1.3	0.7	3.0	26	tr	17
0.4	0.2	0.2	10.2	1.0	0.5	3.0	20	3	13
2.7	0.1	0.3	9.6	1.0	0.3	3.0	17	3	7
2.8	0.4	0.4	12.6	1.4	0.5	4.0	25	7	7
1.1	0.2	0.5	11.2	1.7	0.6	3.0	26	7	13
0.6	0.2	0.1	5.9	0.9	0.1	2.0	5	2	0
n	0.1	0.1	2.7	n	n	tr	4	n	3
0.8	0.1	tr	2.0	0.1	tr	tr	2	1	0
1.4	0.4	0.3	16.2	1.6	0.4	3.0	54	3	8
1.5	0.1	0.1	2.0	0.3	0.1	tr	3	3	tr
n	0.2	0.3	6.8	0.6	0.1	4.0	16	2	0
5.2	0.4	0.7	**56.0**	**7.9**	**2.1**	4.0	56	18	7

FISH AND FISH DISHES

FOOD	AVERAGE PORTION SIZE	TOTAL CALORIES	FAT-SOLUBLE VITAMINS		
			A	D	
	oz per portion	kcals per portion	either Retinol (µg/portion) (QCT: 700µg/day)	or Carotene (µg/portion) (QCT: 4800µg/day)	Cholecalciferol (µg/portion) (QCT: 5µg/day*)
					(*see pages 98–9)
White fish					
Cod, fried in batter	4	239	n	tr	tr
Cod, grilled	4	114	2	tr	tr
Haddock, fried	4	209	tr	tr	tr
Plaice, fried in batter	4	308	n	tr	tr
Skate, fried in batter	4	202	11	tr	n
Sole, flounder, steamed	4	109	tr	tr	tr
Oily fish					
Anchovies, canned	½	29	9	tr	n
Herring, grilled	4	217	41	tr	19.3
Kipper, grilled	4	306	46	tr	11.3
Mackerel, smoked	5	531	47	tr	12.0
Salmon, canned	1 ¾	77	16	tr	4.6
Salmon, grilled	3 ½	215	16	tr	7.1
Salmon, smoked	1 ¾	71	n	tr	n
Sardines, canned	3 ½	172	6	tr	4.6
Sardines, in tomato sauce	1 ¾	72	4	70	7.0
Trout, grilled	4	162	35	tr	11.5
Tuna, canned	3 ½	99	n	tr	3.6
Seafood					
Lobster, boiled	3 ¼	93	tr	tr	tr
Mussels, boiled	1 ½	42	n	tr	tr
Prawns/shrimp, boiled	2	59	tr	tr	tr
Squid (calamare), fried in batter	2 ¼	127	30	tr	0.1
Fish products and dishes					
Cod roe, fried	4	242	90	tr	20.4
Fish sticks	2	143	tr	tr	tr
Pasta with seafood	9	275	130	130	0
Taramasalata	1 ¾	252	n	n	n

E										C
						WATER-SOLUBLE VITAMINS				
							THE B-GROUP			
Tocopherol (mg/portion) (QCI: 15mg/day)	Thiamin B1 (mg/portion) (QCI: 1.1mg/day)	Riboflavin B2 (mg/portion) (QCI: 1.2mg/day)	Niacin B3 (mg/portion) (QCI: 15mg/day)	Pantothenate B5 (mg/portion) (QCI: 5mg/day)	Pyridoxine B6 (mg/portion) (QCI: 1.3mg/day)	Cobalamin B12 (µg/portion) (QCI: 2.4µg/day)	Folate (µg/portion) (QCI: 400µg/day)	Biotin (µg/portion) (QCI: 30µg/day)	Ascorbic acid (mg/portion) (QCI: 75mg/day)	
n	0.1	0.1	4.4	0.4	0.2	2.4	**68**	4	tr	
1.2	0.1	0.1	7.0	0.4	0.3	2.4	12	1	tr	
n	0.1	0.1	6.6	0.3	0.3	1.2	n	2	tr	
n	0.2	0.4	5.5	1.0	0.1	n	32	**36**	tr	
1.4	tr	0.1	6.1	n	n	n	n	n	tr	
n	0.1	0.1	9.1	0.4	0.1	1.2	16	6	tr	
n	tr	tr	1.3	n	n	1.7	3	n	tr	
0.8	tr	0.3	9.4	0.9	0.4	**18.0**	12	8	tr	
0.4	tr	0.3	10.0	0.6	0.3	14.4	6	6	tr	
0.4	0.4	**0.8**	19.5	1.6	**0.8**	9.0	n	5	tr	
0.8	tr	0.1	5.2	0.4	0.1	2.0	7	5	tr	
2.3	0.3	0.1	12.2	1.2	**0.8**	5.0	19	5	tr	
n	0.1	0.1	6.8	0.4	0.1	1.5	1	n	tr	
n	tr	0.3	10.1	0.8	0.2	13.0	8	10	tr	
1.3	tr	0.2	4.5	0.4	0.1	6.5	n	6	tr	
1.2	0.2	0.1	9.8	1.9	0.4	6.0	12	4	tr	
0.6	tr	0.1	18.8	0.3	0.5	4.0	4	2	tr	
1.3	0.1	0.1	5.0	0.9	0.1	2.7	8	6	tr	
0.4	tr	0.2	2.0	0.2	tr	8.8	15	4	tr	
n	tr	0.1	3.1	0.2	tr	4.8	n	1	tr	
1.5	0.1	0.1	2.7	0.3	0.2	1.3	10	n	tr	
n	**0.7**	0.4	5.9	**3.1**	0.3	13.2	n	18	tr	
n	0.1	tr	2.5	0.2	0.1	0.6	10	1	tr	
1.0	0.1	0.2	6.8	0.5	0.2	2.5	15	3	**3**	
n	tr	0.1	0.5	n	n	1.5	2	n	1	

DAIRY PRODUCTS

FOOD	AVERAGE PORTION SIZE	TOTAL CALORIES	FAT-SOLUBLE VITAMINS		
			A	D	
	oz/fl oz per portion	kcals per portion	either Retinol (µg/portion) (QCT: 700µg/day)	or Carotene (µg/portion) (QCT: 4800µg/day)	Cholecalciferol (µg/portion) (QCT: 5µg/day*)	(*see pages 98–9)
Milk					
Skim milk	7	64	tr	tr	tr
Semi-skim (low-fat) milk	7	92	38	tr	tr
Whole (full-fat) milk	7	132	66	40	tr
Goat's milk	7	124	88	tr	tr
Soy milk, unsweetened	7	52	tr	tr	0
Milkshake, thick	7	176	70	22	tr
Cream (2 tbs)					
Light cream	1	58	87	51	4.0
Heavy cream	1	149	234	145	4.0
Crème fraîche	1	113	116	43	4.0
Cheeses					
Brie/camembert	1 ½	137	119	77	3.0
Cheddar/Monterey Jack	1 ½	166	146	56	5.0
Cottage cheese	1 ½	40	18	tr	0
Cream cheese	1 ½	176	154	88	5.0
Edam	1 ½	136	75	73	3.0
Feta	1 ½	100	88	tr	8.0
Goat's cheese, soft	1 ½	128	133	tr	8.0
Gouda	1 ½	151	103	56	3.0
Mozzarella, fresh	1 ½	103	103	61	3.0
Parmesan, fresh	1 ½	166	148	93	5.0
Stilton	1 ½	164	144	73	3.0
Strong blue	1 ½	137	98	113	3.0
Yogurt					
Full-fat yogurt, plain	5	119	42	32	0
Greek-style set yogurt, plain	5	200	173	tr	6.0
Greek-style yogurt, sheep's milk	5	138	129	17	12.0
Soy yogurt, with fruit	5	110	35	tr	0
Fromage frais, plain	3 ½	113	82	tr	0

continues

									WATER-SOLUBLE VITAMINS	
E							THE B-GROUP			**C**
Tocopherol (mg/portion) (QCI: 15mg/day)	Thiamin B1 (mg/portion) (QCI: 1.1mg/day)	Riboflavin B2 (mg/portion) (QCI: 1.2mg/day)	Niacin B3 (mg/portion) (QCI: 15mg/day)	Pantothenate B5 (mg/portion) (QCI: 5mg/day)	Pyridoxine B6 (mg/portion) (QCI: 1.3mg/day)	Cobalamin B12 (µg/portion) (QCI: 2.4µg/day)	Folate (µg/portion) (QCI: 400µg/day)	Biotin (µg/portion) (QCI: 30µg/day)	Ascorbic acid (mg/portion) (QCI: 75mg/day)	
tr	0.1	0.4	1.6	1.0	0.1	1.6	18	5	2	
0.1	0.1	0.5	1.8	0.6	0.1	0.8	12	4	2	
1.6	0.1	0.5	1.6	1.2	0.1	1.8	16	5	**4**	
0.1	0.1	0.1	1.6	0.8	0.1	0.2	2	6	2	
0.6	0.1	0.1	1.6	tr	0.1	0	28	2	0	
0.2	0.1	0.5	1.6	0.6	0.1	1.0	8	4	2	
0.1	tr	0.1	0.2	0.1	tr	0.1	2	1	tr	
0.5	tr	0.1	0.1	0.1	tr	0.2	2	tr	tr	
0.2	tr	0.1	tr	n	tr	0.1	1	n	n	
0.3	tr	0.1	2.0	0.2	0.1	0.2	22	1	tr	
0.2	tr	0.2	2.8	0.2	0.1	1.0	12	2	tr	
0	tr	0.1	1.4	0.1	tr	0.2	9	2	tr	
0.4	tr	0.1	0.3	0.1	tr	0.1	4	1	tr	
0.3	tr	0.1	2.5	0.2	tr	0.8	16	1	tr	
0.1	tr	0.1	1.5	0.1	tr	0.4	9	1	tr	
0.3	tr	0.2	2.7	0.2	tr	0.2	9	2	tr	
0.2	tr	0.1	2.8	0.1	tr	0.7	17	1	tr	
0.1	tr	0.2	2.0	0.1	tr	0.7	8	1	tr	
0.3	tr	0.1	3.6	0.2	tr	1.3	5	1	tr	
0.2	tr	0.2	2.6	0.4	0.1	0.5	31	1	tr	
0.3	tr	0.2	2.4	0.2	tr	0.5	22	1	tr	
0.1	0.1	0.4	2.3	0.8	**0.2**	0.3	27	4	2	
0.6	**0.2**	0.2	2.4	n	tr	0.3	9	n	tr	
1.1	0.1	0.5	1.8	n	0.1	0.3	5	n	tr	
2.9	**0.2**	tr	n	0.2	tr	0	n	2	0	
0.2	0.1	0.2	1.3	0.5	tr	0.5	15	tr	tr	

DAIRY PRODUCTS

FOOD	AVERAGE PORTION SIZE	TOTAL CALORIES	FAT-SOLUBLE VITAMINS			
				A	D	
	oz per portion	kcals per portion	either Retinol (µg/portion) (QCT: 700µg/day)	or Carotene (µg/portion) (QCT: 4800µg/day)	Cholecalciferol (µg/portion) (QCT: 5µg/day*)	(*see pages 98–9)
Ice cream						
Dairy ice cream	3 ½	**215**	164	80	**12.0**	
Non-dairy ice cream	3 ½	**153**	tr	tr	tr	
Eggs and egg dishes						
Egg, boiled	1 ¾	**74**	95	tr	0.9	
Egg, fried	2	**107**	129	tr	0.5	
Egg, scrambled	4	**308**	384	125	0.8	
Omelet	4	**234**	296	64	0.8	
Quiche	4	**378**	221	71	0.4	

	WATER-SOLUBLE VITAMINS								
E	THE B-GROUP								C
Tocopherol (mg/portion) (QCT: 15mg/day)	Thiamin B1 (mg/portion) (QCT: 1.1mg/day)	Riboflavin B2 (mg/portion) (QCT: 1.2mg/day)	Niacin B3 (mg/portion) (QCT: 15mg/day)	Pantothenate B5 (mg/portion) (QCT: 5mg/day)	Pyridoxine B6 (mg/portion) (QCT: 1.3mg/day)	Cobalamin B12 (µg/portion) (QCT: 2.4µg/day)	Folate (µg/portion) (QCT: 400µg/day)	Biotin (µg/portion) (QCT: 30µg/day)	Ascorbic acid (mg/portion) (QCT: 75mg/day)
0.3	0.1	0.3	1.1	1.1	tr	0.5	6	2	1
0.6	0.1	0.3	0.9	0.4	tr	0	8	3	1
0.6	tr	0.2	1.9	0.7	tr	0.6	20	8	0
n	tr	0.2	3.1	0.8	0.1	1.0	24	11	0
1.5	0.1	0.4	3.8	**1.6**	0.1	**2.6**	**36**	20	tr
1.3	0.1	0.4	4.0	**1.6**	0.1	**2.6**	**36**	21	tr
2.7	0.1	0.3	**4.3**	0.7	0.1	1.8	19	9	1

FATS AND OILS

FOOD	AVERAGE PORTION SIZE		TOTAL CALORIES	FAT-SOLUBLE VITAMINS		
				A		D
(amounts in brackets represent size of average portion)	oz/ fl oz per portion		kcals per portion	either Retinol (µg/portion) (QCT: 700µg/day)	or Carotene (µg/portion) (QCT: 4800µg/day)	Cholecalciferol (µg/portion) (QCT: 5µg/day*) *(*see pages 98–9)*
Cooking fats (1 tbs)						
Ghee, butter	1/2		135	101	0	0.1
Ghee, vegetable	1/2		134	tr	tr	0
Lard	1/2		134	tr	tr	n
Suet, beef	1/2		124	8	tr	tr
Suet, vegetable	1/2		125	0	0	0
Table fats (on 1 slice of bread)						
Butter	1/4		74	82	43	0.1
Spread	1/4		68	57	45	0.4
Low-fat spread	1/4		39	16	43	tr
Margarine, hard	1/4		72	67	**75**	0.8
- hard vegetable	1/4		74	67	**75**	0.8
- polyunsaturated	1/4		75	68	35	0.8
Spread (70–80% fat)	1/4		64	n	n	n
- (60% fat)	1/4		55	98	tr	n
- with olive oil	1/4		57	n	n	n
- (35–40% fat)	1/4		37	n	n	n
- (20–25% fat)	1/4		25	47	58	0.8
Oils (1 tbs)						
Cod liver oil	1/2		135	**270**	tr	**31.5**
Corn oil	1/2		135	0	tr	0
Evening primrose oil	1/2		135	0	tr	0
Grapeseed oil	1/2		135	0	tr	0
Olive oil	1/2		135	0	tr	0
Safflower oil	1/2		135	0	tr	0
Sesame oil	1/2		135	0	tr	0
Sunflower oil	1/2		135	0	tr	0
Vegetable oil, blended	1/2		135	0	tr	0
Walnut oil	1/2		135	0	tr	0
Wheat germ oil	1/2		135	0	tr	0

| Tocopherol (mg/portion) (QCT: 15mg/day) | WATER-SOLUBLE VITAMINS | | | | | | | | | C |
| | THE B-GROUP | | | | | | | | | |
E	Thiamin B1 (mg/portion) (QCT: 1.1mg/day)	Riboflavin B2 (mg/portion) (QCT: 1.2mg/day)	Niacin B3 (mg/portion) (QCT: 15mg/day)	Pantothenate B5 (mg/portion) (QCT: 5mg/day)	Pyridoxine B6 (mg/portion) (QCT: 1.3mg/day)	Cobalamin B12 (µg/portion) (QCT: 2.4µg/day)	Folate (µg/portion) (QCT: 400µg/day)	Biotin (µg/portion) (QCT: 30µg/day)	Ascorbic acid (mg/portion) (QCT: 75mg/day)
0.1	tr	tr	tr	tr	tr	tr	tr	tr	0
1.5	tr	tr	tr	tr	tr	tr	tr	tr	0
0.2	tr	tr	tr	tr	tr	tr	tr	tr	0
0.2	tr	tr	tr	tr	tr	tr	tr	tr	0
2.7	tr	tr	tr	tr	tr	tr	tr	tr	0
0.2	tr	tr	tr	tr	tr	tr	tr	tr	0
1.1	tr	tr	tr	tr	tr	tr	tr	tr	0
0.4	tr	tr	tr	tr	tr	tr	tr	tr	0
0.4	tr	tr	tr	tr	tr	tr	tr	tr	0
n	tr	tr	tr	tr	tr	tr	tr	tr	0
3.3	tr	tr	tr	tr	tr	tr	tr	tr	0
3.8	tr	tr	tr	tr	tr	tr	tr	tr	0
3.1	tr	tr	tr	tr	tr	tr	tr	tr	0
n	tr	tr	tr	tr	tr	tr	tr	tr	0
n	tr	tr	tr	tr	tr	tr	tr	tr	0
0.5	tr	tr	tr	tr	tr	tr	tr	tr	0
3.0	tr	tr	tr	tr	tr	tr	tr	tr	0
2.6	tr	tr	tr	tr	tr	tr	tr	tr	0
n	tr	tr	tr	tr	tr	tr	tr	tr	0
n	tr	tr	tr	tr	tr	tr	tr	tr	0
0.8	tr	tr	tr	tr	tr	tr	tr	tr	0
6.1	tr	tr	tr	tr	tr	tr	tr	tr	0
n	tr	tr	tr	tr	tr	tr	tr	tr	0
7.4	tr	tr	tr	tr	tr	tr	tr	tr	0
n	tr	tr	tr	tr	tr	tr	tr	tr	0
n	tr	tr	tr	tr	tr	tr	tr	tr	0
20.5	tr	tr	tr	tr	tr	tr	tr	tr	0

GRAINS, CEREALS, BREADS

FOOD	AVERAGE PORTION SIZE	TOTAL CALORIES	FAT-SOLUBLE VITAMINS			
				A	D	
	oz per portion	kcals per portion	either Retinol (µg/portion) (QCT: 700µg/day)	or Carotene (µg/portion) (QCT: 4800µg/day)	Cholecalciferol (µg/portion) (QCT: 5µg/day*)	(*see pages 98–9)
Flours and grains						
Barley, pearl	3 ½	360	0	0	0	
Buckwheat	3 ½	364	0	0	0	
Bulgur wheat	3 ½	353	0	n	0	
Cornstarch	3 ½	354	0	0	0	
Couscous	3 ½	227	0	tr	0	
Custard powder	3 ½	354	0	0	0	
Millet	3 ½	354	0	0	0	
Oatmeal	3 ½	401	0	0	0	
Quinoa	3 ½	309	0	n	0	
Rice, brown	7	282	0	0	0	
Rice, white	7	276	0	0	0	
Rice flour	3 ½	366	0	0	0	
Rye flour	3 ½	335	0	0	0	
Soy flour	3 ½	447	0	n	0	
Wheat flour, white	3 ½	341	0	0	0	
Wheat flour, wholewheat	3 ½	310	0	0	0	
Wheat germ	¾	76	0	0	0	
Wheat bran	½	31	0	3	0	
Noodles and pasta (cooked)						
Noodles, egg	10	186	6	0	0	
Noodles, plain	10	186	0	0	0	
Pasta, white	10	312	0	0	0	
Pasta, wholewheat	10	339	0	0	0	
Pastry						
Puff pastry	3 ½	373	0	0	n	
Shortcrust pastry	3 ½	449	120	0	1.2	
Breakfast cereals						
All-bran	1 ¾	126	0	11	1.4	
Coco pops	1 ¾	193	0	11	1.4	

continues

| | WATER-SOLUBLE VITAMINS | | | | | | | | |
| E | | | THE B-GROUP | | | | | | C |
Tocopherol (mg/portion) (QCT: 15mg/day)	Thiamin B1 (mg/portion) (QCT: 1.1mg/day)	Riboflavin B2 (mg/portion) (QCT: 1.2mg/day)	Niacin B3 (mg/portion) (QCT: 15mg/day)	Pantothenate B5 (mg/portion) (QCT: 5mg/day)	Pyridoxine B6 (mg/portion) (QCT: 1.3mg/day)	Cobalamin B12 (µg/portion) (QCT: 2.4µg/day)	Folate (µg/portion) (QCT: 400µg/day)	Biotin (µg/portion) (QCT: 30µg/day)	Ascorbic acid (mg/portion) (QCT: 75mg/day)
0.4	0.1	0.1	0.1	0.5	0.2	0	20	tr	0
tr	0.3	0.1	4.5	1.2	0.4	0	n	n	0
n	0.5	0.1	6.1	n	n	0	n	n	0
tr	tr	tr	tr	tr	tr	0	tr	tr	0
n	0.2	0.1	1.9	n	n	0	n	n	0
tr	tr	tr	tr	tr	tr	0	tr	tr	0
tr	0.7	0.2	2.8	n	n	0	n	n	0
1.5	0.9	0.1	3.4	1.2	0.3	0	60	**21**	0
n	0.2	0.4	4.8	n	n	0	n	n	0
0.6	0.3	tr	3.8	n	n	0	20	n	0
tr	tr	tr	3.0	tr	0.1	0	8	2	0
n	0.1	0.1	3.5	n	0.2	0	n	n	0
1.6	0.4	0.2	2.6	1.0	0.4	0	78	6	0
1.5	0.8	0.3	**10.6**	**1.6**	0.5	0	**345**	n	0
0.3	0.3	tr	3.6	0.3	0.2	0	22	1	0
1.4	0.5	0.1	8.3	0.1	0.5	0	57	7	0
5.5	0.5	0.2	2.5	0.5	0.8	0	83	6	0
0.4	0.1	0.1	4.9	0.4	0.2	0	39	7	0
n	tr	tr	2.1	n	tr	tr	3	n	0
tr	0.1	tr	2.4	tr	tr	0	6	tr	0
tr	tr	tr	3.6	tr	0.1	0	12	tr	0
tr	0.6	0.1	6.9	0.6	0.2	0	21	tr	0
n	0.2	tr	2.1	n	0.1	tr	16	n	0
1.4	0.2	tr	2.1	0.2	0.1	0	13	1	0
0.1	0.2	0.1	3.0	0.3	0.1	0	31	3	0
0.1	0.2	0.1	3.0	0.3	0.1	0	31	3	0

GRAINS, CEREALS, BREADS

FOOD	AVERAGE PORTION SIZE	TOTAL CALORIES	FAT-SOLUBLE VITAMINS			
				A	D	
(where appropriate, numbers in brackets represent number of items in average portion)	oz per portion	kcals per portion	either Retinol (µg/portion) (QCI: 700µg/day)	or Carotene (µg/portion) (QCI: 4800µg/day)	Cholecalciferol (µg/portion) (QCI: 5µg/day*)	(*see pages 98–9)
Corn flakes	1 ¾	178	0	11	1.4	
Fruit 'n' Fibre	1 ¾	176	0	11	1.4	
Grapenuts	1 ¾	173	0	11	2.2	
Muesli (Swiss style)	2 ½	255	0	15	0	
Porridge (made with water)	7	98	0	0	0	
Puffed wheat	1 ¾	161	0	11	0	
Rice Krispies	1 ¾	185	0	11	1.4	
Shredded wheat (2)	1 ¾	163	0	11	0	
Special K	1 ¾	190	0	11	1.4	
Weetabix (2)	1 ½	142	0	8	0	
Breads and rolls						
Bagel (1)	3 ¼	246	0	19	2.5	
Brown bread (1 slice)	1 ½	87	0	8	0	
Chapati (1)	2	111	0	12	0	
French stick (2 in slice)	1 ½	108	0	8	0	
Granary bread (1 slice)	1 ½	94	0	8	0	
Naan bread (1)	5 ½	538	155	0	0.3	
Papadum (fried) (2)	¾	96	0	n	0	
Pita bread (1 large)	3 ½	252	0	0	0	
Rye bread (1 slice)	¾	55	0	0	0	
Wheat germ bread (1 slice)	1 ½	105	0	8	0	
White bread (1 slice)	1 ½	94	0	8	0	
Wholewheat bread (1 slice)	1 ½	86	0	8	0	
Croissant (1)	1 ¾	180	11	11	0.1	
Hamburger bun (1)	1 ¾	132	n	0	n	
Soft white roll (1)	1 ¾	135	0	11	0	
Wholewheat roll (1)	1 ¾	121	0	11	0	

| | WATER-SOLUBLE VITAMINS | | | | | | | | |
| E | | | | THE B-GROUP | | | | | C |
Tocopherol (mg/portion) (QCI: 15mg/day)	Thiamin B1 (mg/portion) (QCI: 1.1mg/day)	Riboflavin B2 (mg/portion) (QCI: 1.2mg/day)	Niacin B3 (mg/portion) (QCI: 15mg/day)	Pantothenate B5 (mg/portion) (QCI: 5mg/day)	Pyridoxine B6 (mg/portion) (QCI: 1.3mg/day)	Cobalamin B12 (µg/portion) (QCI: 2.4µg/day)	Folate (µg/portion) (QCI: 400µg/day)	Biotin (µg/portion) (QCI: 30µg/day)	Ascorbic acid (mg/portion) (QCI: 75mg/day)
0.1	0.2	0.1	0	0.3	0.1	0	31	3	0
0.1	0.2	0.1	3.0	0.3	0.1	0	31	3	0
0.1	0.2	0.1	3.0	0.3	0.1	0	31	3	0
0.1	0.2	0.1	4.1	0.4	0.1	0	43	4	0
0.4	**1.2**	tr	0.8	0.2	tr	0	8	4	0
1.0	tr	tr	4.1	0.3	0.1	0	10	4	0
0.3	0.5	0.8	8.7	0.4	0.9	1.0	125	1	0
0.6	0.1	tr	3.3	0.4	0.1	0	15	5	0
0.3	0.6	0.9	10.6	0.3	1.1	1.0	150	2	0
0.4	0.3	0.4	4.8	0.3	0.1	0	20	3	0
0.5	0.9	**1.4**	**15.7**	0.6	**1.6**	**2**	225	2	0
tr	0.1	tr	1.7	0.1	0.1	0	16	1	0
tr	0.1	tr	1.7	0.1	0.1	0	8	1	0
0.1	0.1	tr	2.4	0.2	0.1	0	16	2	0
n	0.1	tr	2.0	n	0.1	0	36	n	tr
2.2	0.3	0.2	4.8	0.5	0.1	tr	22	3	0
n	tr	tr	0.9	n	n	0	7	n	0
n	0.2	0.1	3.2	n	n	0	20	n	0
0.3	0.1	tr	1.0	0.1	tr	0	6	n	0
n	0.2	tr	2.0	0.1	0.1	0	18	1	0
tr	0.1	tr	1.4	0.1	tr	0	12	0	0
tr	0.1	tr	1.3	0.1	tr	0	10	0	0
tr	0.1	0.1	1.9	0.3	0.1	tr	37	5	0
tr	0.1	tr	1.7	0.2	tr	tr	24	1	0
tr	0.1	tr	2.2	0.2	tr	0	16	1	0
0.1	0.2	0.1	3.0	0.3	0.1	0	31	3	0

BISCUITS, CAKES, DESSERTS

FOOD	AVERAGE PORTION SIZE	TOTAL CALORIES	FAT-SOLUBLE VITAMINS			
				A	D	
(where appropriate, numbers in brackets represent number of items in average portion)	oz per portion	kcals per portion	either Retinol (µg/portion) (QCT: 700µg/day)	or Carotene (µg/portion) (QCT: 4800µg/day)	Cholecalciferol (µg/portion) (QCT: 5µg/day*)	(*see pages 98–9)
Biscuits and cookies						
Chocolate cookie (1)	¾	131	tr	5	0	
Cream cracker (1)	½	66	0	3	0	
Crispbread, rye (1)	½	32	0	2	0	
Flapjack (oatmeal cookie) (1)	2	290	138	13	1.4	
Graham cracker (1)	½	71	0	3	0	
Oatcake (1)	½	66	0	3	0	
Plain cookie (1)	½	46	0	2	0	
Plain cracker (1)	½	44	0	2	0	
Shortbread (1)	½	75	41	3	tr	
Wholewheat cookie (1)	½	54	12	3	0.1	
Wholewheat cracker (1)	½	62	0	3	0	
Cakes						
Chocolate cake (1 slice)	2 ½	319	189	15	1.7	
Fruit cake (1 slice)	2 ½	248	n	15	n	
Gâteau (1 slice)	2 ½	236	221	0	0.4	
Sponge cake (1 slice)	2 ½	321	196	15	**1.8**	
Jelly roll (1 slice)	1 ¼	97	28	7	0.2	
Desserts						
Cheesecake (1 slice)	3 ¾	452	**385**	n	1.0	
Christmas pudding	3 ½	291	25	n	0.1	
Fruit crisp/cobbler	6	337	n	n	1.1	
Custard sauce (made with milk)	5	176	96	n	tr	
Fruit pie	4	223	56	n	0.4	
Pancake (1)	3 ¾	331	64	n	0.2	
Rice pudding	7	178	n	n	n	
Trifle	6	272	128	n	0.2	
Buns and pastries						
Crumpet (1)	1 ½	71	0	0	0	
Currant bun (1)	2	178	n	n	0	

continues

| E | WATER-SOLUBLE VITAMINS | | | | | | | | C |
| | THE B-GROUP | | | | | | | | |
Tocopherol (mg/portion) (QCI: 15mg/day)	Thiamin B1 (mg/portion) (QCI: 1.1mg/day)	Riboflavin B2 (mg/portion) (QCI: 1.2mg/day)	Niacin B3 (mg/portion) (QCI: 15mg/day)	Pantothenate B5 (mg/portion) (QCI: 5mg/day)	Pyridoxine B6 (mg/portion) (QCI: 1.3mg/day)	Cobalamin B12 (µg/portion) (QCI: 2.4µg/day)	Folate (µg/portion) (QCI: 400µg/day)	Biotin (µg/portion) (QCI: 30µg/day)	Ascorbic acid (mg/portion) (QCI: 75mg/day)
0.4	tr	tr	0.4	n	tr	0	n	n	0
0.2	tr	tr	0.5	tr	tr	0	3	tr	0
0.1	tr	tr	0.3	0.1	tr	0	4	1	0
1.7	0.2	tr	0.8	0.2	0.1	0	7	5	0
n	tr	tr	0.4	n	tr	0	2	n	0
0.3	0.1	tr	0.5	0.2	tr	0	4	3	0
0.1	tr	tr	0.3	n	tr	0	1	n	0
n	tr	tr	0.3	n	tr	0	n	n	0
0.1	tr	tr	0.3	tr	tr	0	1	tr	0
0.3	0.1	tr	1.1	0.1	0.1	tr	4	1	0
0.2	tr	tr	0.7	0.1	tr	0	4	1	0
1.9	0.1	0.1	1.8	0.4	tr	0.7	8	6	0
n	0.1	0.1	1.1	n	n	0	n	n	0
n	0.1	0.2	1.5	0.4	tr	0.9	9	7	0
2.0	0.1	0.1	1.8	0.4	tr	0.7	7	5	0
0.3	tr	0.1	0.8	0.2	tr	0.4	5	4	tr
n	tr	0.2	1.7	n	tr	tr	8	n	1
0.6	0.1	0.1	1.7	0.2	0.1	tr	8	4	0
1.7	0.1	tr	1.5	0.2	0.1	0	5	tr	5
0.2	0.1	**0.3**	1.5	0.6	0.1	**1.5**	9	3	2
0.8	0.1	tr	1.1	0.1	tr	0	4	tr	6
0.4	0.1	0.2	2.1	0.6	0.1	1.1	9	6	1
n	0.1	**0.3**	1.8	n	tr	tr	n	n	0
0.7	0.1	0.2	2.0	0.5	0.1	tr	15	5	**7**
0.1	0.1	tr	0.8	0.1	tr	tr	3	2	0
n	0.2	0.1	1.3	n	0.1	tr	24	n	0

BISCUITS, CAKES, DESSERTS

FOOD	AVERAGE PORTION SIZE	TOTAL CALORIES	FAT-SOLUBLE VITAMINS		
				A	D
(where appropriate, numbers in brackets represent number of items in average portion)	oz per portion	kcals per portion	either Retinol (µg/portion) (QCT: 700µg/day)	or Carotene (µg/portion) (QCT: 4800µg/day)	Cholecalciferol (µg/portion) (QCT: 5µg/day*)	(*see pages 98–9)
Danish pastry (1)	3 ¾	411	n	n	n
Doughnut (jelly) (1)	2 ½	252	n	n	n
Greek pastry (Baklava) (1)	3 ½	322	n	0	n
Hot cross bun (1)	1 ¾	155	34	11	0.3
Muffin (American) (1)	2 ½	256	0	15	0
Muffin (English) (1)	2 ½	198	47	15	0.3
Scone (1)	1 ¾	181	70	11	0.6
Teacake (1)	2	178	n	13	0
Waffle (1)	2 ¼	217	130	14	0.2

| E | WATER-SOLUBLE VITAMINS | | | | | | | | | | C |
| | | | | | THE B-GROUP | | | | | |
Tocopherol (mg/portion) (QCI: 15mg/day)	Thiamin B1 (mg/portion) (QCI: 1.1mg/day)	Riboflavin B2 (mg/portion) (QCI: 1.2mg/day)	Niacin B3 (mg/portion) (QCI: 15mg/day)	Pantothenate B5 (mg/portion) (QCI: 5mg/day)	Pyridoxine B6 (mg/portion) (QCI: 1.3mg/day)	Cobalamin B12 (µg/portion) (QCI: 2.4µg/day)	Folate (µg/portion) (QCI: 400µg/day)	Biotin (µg/portion) (QCI: 30µg/day)	Ascorbic acid (mg/portion) (QCI: 75mg/day)
tr	0.1	0.1	2.3	0.6	0.1	tr	22	**8**	0
tr	0.2	0.1	1.9	n	0.1	tr	16	n	n
n	0.1	tr	2.0	n	n	n	n	n	n
0.4	0.1	0.1	1.4	0.2	0.1	tr	14	3	0
0.8	0.2	tr	**4.6**	0.6	**0.2**	0	20	6	0
0.5	0.1	0.1	2.7	0.4	0.1	tr	**32**	5	tr
0.7	0.1	tr	1.3	0.1	0.1	tr	4	1	tr
n	0.1	0.1	2.0	n	tr	tr	22	n	tr
0.5	0.1	0.1	1.8	0.3	0.1	0.7	7	4	1

SUGAR PRODUCTS

FOOD (where appropriate, numbers in brackets represent size of average portion)	AVERAGE PORTION SIZE oz per portion	TOTAL CALORIES kcals per portion	FAT-SOLUBLE VITAMINS			
			A		D	
			either Retinol (µg/portion) (QCT: 700µg/day)	or Carotene (µg/portion) (QCT: 4800µg/day)	Cholecalciferol (µg/portion) (QCT: 5µg/day*)	(**see pages 98–9)
Sugars and syrups (1 tbs)						
Honey	¹/₂	58	0	0	0	
Molasses	¹/₂	53	0	0	0	
Sugar, brown	¹/₂	72	0	0	0	
Sugar, white	¹/₂	79	0	0	0	
Syrup, light corn	¹/₂	60	0	0	0	
Syrup, maple	¹/₂	52	0	0	0	
Treacle, black	¹/₂	51	0	0	0	
Preserves and spreads (1 tbs)						
Chocolate nut spread	¹/₂	110	0	288	0	
Fruit spread	¹/₂	24	0	53	0	
Jelly	¹/₂	52	0	46	0	
Chocolate						
Chocolate bar	1 ³/₄	221	4	20	tr	
Milk chocolate	1 ³/₄	260	13	tr	0	
Plain chocolate	1 ³/₄	255	8	tr	0	
Confectionery						
Hard candy	1 ³/₄	164	0	0	0	
Cereal crunchy bar	1 ³/₄	234	0	tr	0	
Fruit pastilles	1 ³/₄	164	0	0	0	
Halva (with carrot)	1 ³/₄	177	70	4,715	0.2	
Liquorice shapes	1 ³/₄	139	0	0	0	
Nougat	1 ³/₄	192	0	10	0	
Peppermints	1 ³/₄	197	0	0	0	
Turkish delight (with nuts)	1 ³/₄	172	0	tr	0	

| E | | | | | | WATER-SOLUBLE VITAMINS | | | C |
| | | | | | | THE B-GROUP | | | |
Tocopherol (mg/portion) (QCT: 15mg/day)	Thiamin B1 (mg/portion) (QCT: 1.1mg/day)	Riboflavin B2 (mg/portion) (QCT: 1.2mg/day)	Niacin B3 (mg/portion) (QCT: 15mg/day)	Pantothenate B5 (mg/portion) (QCT: 5mg/day)	Pyridoxine B6 (mg/portion) (QCT: 1.3mg/day)	Cobalamin B12 (µg/portion) (QCT: 2.4µg/day)	Folate (µg/portion) (QCT: 400µg/day)	Biotin (µg/portion) (QCT: 30µg/day)	Ascorbic acid (mg/portion) (QCT: 75mg/day)
tr	tr	tr	tr	n	n	0	n	n	0
0.1	tr	tr	0.2	0	0.1	0	0	tr	0
0	tr	tr	tr	tr	tr	0	tr	tr	0
0	0	0	0	0	0	0	0	0	0
0	tr	tr	tr	0	tr	0	tr	tr	0
0	tr	tr	tr	tr	tr	0	0	tr	0
0	tr	tr	tr	tr	tr	0	tr	tr	0
0.5	0.1	tr	0.5	0.1	tr	0	3	n	tr
0.4	tr	tr	0.4	tr	tr	0	3	tr	1
0.6	tr	tr	0.3	0.1	tr	0	5	n	**2**
0.5	tr	0.1	0.6	0.3	tr	tr	5	1	0
0.2	tr	**0.3**	1.4	**0.4**	tr	**0.5**	6	**2**	0
0.7	tr	tr	0.6	0.2	tr	0	6	**2**	0
0	0	0	0	0	0	0	0	0	0
1.9	0.1	0.1	**3.4**	n	0.1	0	**8**	n	tr
0	0	0	0	0	0	0	0	0	0
0.6	0.1	0.1	0.7	0.3	0.1	0	7	**2**	tr
0	0.1	tr	1.1	n	**0.3**	0	5	n	0
0.3	0.1	0.1	0.7	tr	tr	0	6	n	0
0	0	0	0	0	0	0	0	0	0
0.1	tr	tr	0.2	tr	0	0	2	tr	0

SOUPS AND SAUCES

FOOD	AVERAGE PORTION SIZE	TOTAL CALORIES	FAT-SOLUBLE VITAMINS			
			A		D	
	fl oz per portion	kcals per portion	either Retinol (µg/portion) (QCI: 700µg/day)	or Carotene (µg/portion) (QCI: 4800µg/day)	Cholecalciferol (µg/portion) (QCI: 5µg/day*)	(*see pages 98–9)
Soups (1 cup)						
Bouillabaisse	9	338	tr	0	tr	
Carrot and orange soup	9	50	0	2	0	
Chicken soup	9	145	98	0	tr	
French onion soup	9	100	0	0	0	
Gazpacho	9	113	0	n	0	
Leek and potato soup	9	130	0	0	0	
Lentil soup	9	293	0	0	0	
Minestrone soup	9	158	33	0	tr	
Mushroom soup	9	115	100	0	0	
Oxtail soup	9	110	0	0	0	
Tomato soup	9	130	0	0	0	
Vegetable soup	9	130	0	1	0	
Sauces						
Black bean sauce	1	28	0	n	0	
Brown sauce (spicy)	1	36	0	tr	0	
Curry sauce	4	90	0	n	0	
Dressing, Thousand Island	1	97	4	0	0	
Dressing, yogurt-based	1	88	n	0	n	
Gravy (instant)	2 ½	24	n	0	0	
Hollandaise sauce	2 ½	495	574	0	0.5	
Mayonnaise	1	207	26	0	0	
Mint sauce	½	10	2	tr	0	
Raita	1 ¾	29	10	0	0	
Soy sauce	½	4	0	0	0	
Sweet and sour sauce	5	66	0	n	0	
Tomato ketchup	1	35	0	0	0	
Vinaigrette	1	139	0	0	0	

| | | WATER-SOLUBLE VITAMINS | | | | | | | |
| E | | THE B-GROUP | | | | | | | C |
Tocopherol (mg/portion) (QCT: 15mg/day)	Thiamin B1 (mg/portion) (QCT: 1.1mg/day)	Riboflavin B2 (mg/portion) (QCT: 1.2mg/day)	Niacin B3 (mg/portion) (QCT: 15mg/day)	Pantothenate B5 (mg/portion) (QCT: 5mg/day)	Pyridoxine B6 (mg/portion) (QCT: 1.3mg/day)	Cobalamin B12 (µg/portion) (QCT: 2.4µg/day)	Folate (µg/portion) (QCT: 400µg/day)	Biotin (µg/portion) (QCT: 30µg/day)	Ascorbic acid (mg/portion) (QCT: 75mg/day)
n	n	n	n	n	n	n	n	n	8
0.6	0.1	tr	0.5	0.3	0.1	0	10	tr	5
1.4	tr	0.1	1.3	0.1	tr	tr	3	0	0
0.4	0.1	tr	0.3	tr	0.1	0	5	3	13
2.3	0.1	tr	1.3	0.4	0.2	0	25	3	**28**
0.7	0.2	0.1	1.3	0.4	**0.3**	tr	**30**	3	8
n	0.2	0.1	1.3	**0.9**	**0.3**	0	15	n	3
0.8	0.1	tr	1.5	0.3	0.2	tr	23	tr	13
1.4	tr	0.1	1.3	0.3	tr	tr	5	3	0
0.5	0.1	0.1	**3.0**	0.1	0.1	0	3	0	0
3.5	0.1	0.1	1.5	0.3	0.2	tr	**30**	3	tr
0.6	0.2	tr	0.5	0.3	0.2	0	18	tr	8
n	**0.3**	tr	0.5	n	n	tr	n	n	tr
n	tr	tr	0.1	n	tr	0	2	n	tr
n	tr	tr	0.3	n	tr	0	n	n	0
2.4	tr	tr	0.1	tr	tr	0	1	tr	tr
n	n	n	n	n	n	0	0	n	tr
n	n	n	n	n	n	0	0	n	0
1.7	tr	0.1	1.1	0.7	tr	**1.4**	12	**9**	0
5.7	tr	tr	0.1	n	tr	0.3	1	n	tr
tr	tr	tr	tr	tr	tr	0	tr	tr	tr
0	tr	0.1	0.6	0.2	tr	0	8	1	1
n	tr	tr	0.5	n	n	0	1	n	0
n	0.2	tr	tr	n	n	0	n	n	n
n	**0.3**	tr	0.7	n	tr	0	tr	n	1
n	0	0	0	tr	0	0	0	0	0

PICKLES AND SAVOURIES

FOOD	AVERAGE PORTION SIZE	TOTAL CALORIES	FAT-SOLUBLE VITAMINS			
				A	D	
(where appropriate, numbers in brackets represent number of items in average portion)	oz per portion	kcals per portion	either Retinol (µg/portion) (QCT: 700µg/day)	or Carotene (µg/portion) (QCT: 4800µg/day)	Cholecalciferol (µg/portion) (QCT: 5µg/day*)	(*see pages 98–9)
Pickles and chutneys						
Lime pickle	1 1/2	71	0	39	0	
Piccalilli	1 1/2	34	0	n	0	
Relish (corn/cucumber/onion)	1 1/2	48	0	n	0	
Sweet mango chutney	1 1/2	76	0	52	0	
Tomato chutney	1 1/2	51	0	156	0	
Tomatoes, sun-dried	1 3/4	248	0	**200**	0	
Savoury snacks						
Breadsticks (grissini) (3)	3/4	78	0	tr	0	
Popcorn, plain	1 3/4	297	0	69	0	
Potato chips	1 1/2	212	0	tr	0	
Potato chips, low-fat	1 1/2	183	0	tr	0	
Pretzels	1 3/4	191	0	0	0	
Tortilla chips	1 3/4	230	0	114	0	

| E | | | | | WATER-SOLUBLE VITAMINS | | | | C |
| | | | | | THE B-GROUP | | | | |
Tocopherol (mg/portion) (QCT: 15mg/day)	Thiamin B1 (mg/portion) (QCT: 1.1mg/day)	Riboflavin B2 (mg/portion) (QCT: 1.2mg/day)	Niacin B3 (mg/portion) (QCT: 15mg/day)	Pantothenate B5 (mg/portion) (QCT: 5mg/day)	Pyridoxine B6 (mg/portion) (QCT: 1.3mg/day)	Cobalamin B12 (µg/portion) (QCT: 2.4µg/day)	Folate (µg/portion) (QCT: 400µg/day)	Biotin (µg/portion) (QCT: 30µg/day)	Ascorbic acid (mg/portion) (QCT: 75mg/day)
n	tr	tr	0.3	n	n	0	n	n	tr
n	tr	tr	0.1	n	tr	0	n	tr	tr
n	n	n	n	n	n	0	n	n	n
n	0	tr	0.4	n	n	0	n	n	tr
0.4	tr	0.1	0.4	0.1	0.1	0	7	**1**	2
12.0	n	n	n	n	n	0	n	n	tr
0.1	tr	tr	1.1	0.1	tr	tr	4	tr	tr
3.3	0.1	tr	0.5	0.1	0.1	0	3	**1**	0
2.3	0.1	tr	1.8	**0.4**	**0.3**	0	15	n	2
1.4	0.1	0.1	2.6	n	0.2	0	**19**	n	**6**
n	**0.2**	**0.3**	**2.7**	0.1	0.1	0	n	n	0
1.0	0.1	tr	0.9	n	0.2	0	10	n	tr

DRINKS

FOOD	AVERAGE PORTION SIZE	TOTAL CALORIES	FAT-SOLUBLE VITAMINS		
				A	D
(where appropriate, numbers in brackets represent size of average portion)	fl oz per portion	kcals per portion	either Retinol (µg/portion) (QCT: 700µg/day)	or Carotene (µg/portion) (QCT: 4800µg/day)	Cholecalciferol (µg/portion) (QCT: 5µg/day*)	(*see pages 98–9)
Fruit juices (unsweetened)					
Apple juice	7	76	0	tr	0
Cranberry juice	7	122	0	42	5.6
Grape juice	7	92	0	tr	0
Grapefruit juice	7	66	0	tr	0
Lemon juice (2 tsp)	³/₄	1	0	tr	0
Lime juice (2 tsp)	³/₄	2	0	tr	0
Mango juice	7	78	0	420	0
Orange juice	7	66	0	34	0
Passionfruit juice	7	94	0	1,600	0
Pineapple juice	7	82	0	16	0
Pomegranate juice	7	88	0	66	0
Prune juice	7	114	0	n	0
Hot drinks					
Coffee, black	7	4	0	0	0
Coffee, with milk	7	13	11	2	tr
Coffee, Irish	7	160	n	101	tr
Drinking chocolate (for 1 mug)	¹/₂	66	0	n	0
Tea, black	7	tr	0	0	0
Tea, with milk	7	15	11	tr	0
Tea, green	7	tr	0	0	0
Tea, herbal	7	2	n	0	0
Soft drinks (carbonated)					
Cola	11	129	0	0	0
Fruit juice drink	11	129	0	310	0
Ginger beer	9	38	0	0	0
Lemonade	7	44	0	tr	0
Sports drinks	7	120	0	1,670	0
Tonic water	9	83	0	0	0

continues

								WATER-SOLUBLE VITAMINS		
E								**THE B-GROUP**		**C**
Tocopherol (mg/portion) (QCI: 15mg/day)	Thiamin B1 (mg/portion) (QCI: 1.1mg/day)	Riboflavin B2 (mg/portion) (QCI: 1.2mg/day)	Niacin B3 (mg/portion) (QCI: 15mg/day)	Pantothenate B5 (mg/portion) (QCI: 5mg/day)	Pyridoxine B6 (mg/portion) (QCI: 1.3mg/day)	Cobalamin B12 (µg/portion) (QCI: 2.4µg/day)	Folate (µg/portion) (QCI: 400µg/day)	Biotin (µg/portion) (QCI: 30µg/day)	Ascorbic acid (mg/portion) (QCI: 75mg/day)
tr	tr	tr	0.2	0.1	tr	0	8	2	28
1.1	**2.4**	**3.4**	**42.2**	1.0	**4.4**	**4**	**600**	6	0
tr	tr	tr	0.2	0.1	0.1	0	2	1	tr
0.4	0.1	tr	0.4	0.2	tr	0	12	2	62
n	tr	tr	tr	tr	tr	0	3	tr	7
n	tr	tr	tr	tr	tr	0	n	n	8
2.1	tr	tr	1.0	n	n	0	n	n	50
0.3	0.2	tr	0.6	0.3	0.1	0	56	2	96
n	tr	0.1	1.6	n	n	0	n	n	42
0.1	0.1	tr	0.4	0.1	0.1	0	16	tr	22
n	tr	0.1	0.4	**1.1**	0.6	0	n	n	16
n	tr	0.1	1.4	n	0.3	0	tr	n	tr
tr	tr	tr	1.3	tr	tr	0	tr	**6**	0
tr	0.1	tr	1.3	0.1	tr	tr	2	**6**	0
0.3	0.1	0.1	1.0	0.1	tr	tr	2	4	0
tr	tr	tr	0.4	n	tr	0	2	n	0
n	tr	tr	0	0.1	tr	0	6	2	0
tr	0	0.1	0	0.1	tr	tr	6	2	0
n	0	tr	0.2	tr	tr	0	tr	tr	6
n	tr	tr	0	tr	0	0	2	0	0
0	0	0	0	0	0	0	0	0	0
tr	tr	tr	tr	tr	tr	0	3	tr	3
0	0	0	0	0	0	0	0	0	0
tr	0	0	0	tr	tr	0	tr	tr	tr
0	0	0	0	tr	tr	0	2	tr	16
0	0	0	0	0	0	0	0	0	0

DRINKS

FOOD	AVERAGE PORTION SIZE	TOTAL CALORIES	FAT-SOLUBLE VITAMINS			
			A		D	
	fl oz per portion	kcals per portion	either Retinol (µg/portion) (QCT: 700µg/day)	or Carotene (µg/portion) (QCT: 4800µg/day)	Cholecalciferol (µg/portion) (QCT: 5µg/day*)	(*see pages 98–9)
Soft drinks (uncarbonated)						
Barley water (diluted)	7	28	0	250	0	
Fruit juice drink (diluted)	7	74	0	n	0	
Rosehip syrup (diluted)	7	92	0	200	0	
Alcoholic drinks						
Beer, dark	10	177	0	tr	0	
Beer, lager	10	384	0	tr	0	
Beer, shandy	10	48	0	tr	0	
Beer, stout (eg. Guinness)	10	156	0	tr	0	
Cider	10	108	0	tr	0	
Champagne	4 ½	95	0	tr	0	
Red wine	4 ½	85	0	tr	0	
White wine	4 ½	83	0	tr	0	
Port	2	79	0	tr	0	
Sherry	2	58	0	tr	0	
Vermouth/martini	2	55	0	tr	0	
Cream liqueurs (eg. Kahlua)	¾	81	48	23	tr	
Liqueurs, high-strength (eg. Grand Marnier)	¾	79	0	tr	0	
Liqueurs, med.-strength (eg. campari)	¾	66	0	tr	0	
Spirits (eg. brandy/gin/whiskey)	¾	56	0	0	0	

	WATER-SOLUBLE VITAMINS									
E						THE B-GROUP				**C**
Tocopherol (mg/portion) (QCT: 15mg/day)	Thiamin B1 (mg/portion) (QCT: 1.1mg/day)	Riboflavin B2 (mg/portion) (QCT: 1.2mg/day)	Niacin B3 (mg/portion) (QCT: 15mg/day)	Pantothenate B5 (mg/portion) (QCT: 5mg/day)	Pyridoxine B6 (mg/portion) (QCT: 1.3mg/day)	Cobalamin B12 (µg/portion) (QCT: 2.4µg/day)	Folate (µg/portion) (QCT: 400µg/day)	Biotin (µg/portion) (QCT: 30µg/day)	Ascorbic acid (mg/portion) (QCT: 75mg/day)
n	0	0	tr	0	0	0	0	0	4
n	tr	tr	0.2	tr	tr	0	4	tr	14
0	0	0	0	0	0	0	0	0	**118**
n	tr	0.1	1.2	0.3	0.2	tr	9	3	0
n	tr	0.1	3.0	0.1	0.2	tr	36	3	0
n	tr	tr	0.3	0.1	tr	tr	3	tr	0
n	tr	0.1	3.0	0.1	tr	tr	18	3	0
n	tr	tr	0	0.1	tr	tr	n	3	0
n	tr	tr	0.1	tr	tr	tr	tr	n	0
n	tr	tr	0.1	0.1	tr	tr	1	3	0
n	tr	tr	0	tr	tr	tr	tr	n	0
0	tr	tr	tr	n	tr	tr	tr	n	0
0	tr	tr	tr	n	tr	tr	tr	n	0
0	tr	tr	0	n	tr	tr	tr	n	0
0.1	n	n	n	n	n	0	tr	n	0
0	tr	tr	tr	tr	tr	tr	tr	tr	0
0	tr	tr	tr	tr	tr	tr	tr	tr	0
0	0	0	0	0	0	0	0	0	0

All about minerals

CALCIUM

Calcium gives strength to bones and teeth, which together contain 99 per cent of the calcium in the body. It is also important for the health of the heart, muscles, and nerves, and is a component of various enzymes and hormones. Calcium is abundant in food, and is also found in hard drinking water.

The skeleton acts like a calcium "bank," ensuring that there is always enough available to support vital functions. "Deposits" and "withdrawals" are controlled by hormones,

Calcium TOP 10 (milligrams per 100 grams of food)

FDA recommended intake = 1000 mg/day; 1200 mg/day for over-50s.
Toxicity level = not defined

1.	parmesan cheese	1025	7.	purple-sprouting	
2.	sesame seeds	670		broccoli	200
3.	tofu	510	8.	okra, chick peas,	
4.	cheese (on average)	450		brazil nuts	160
5.	anchovies, sardines	420	9.	beet greens, spinach,	
6.	dried figs, almonds,			curly kale	170
	yogurt	250	10.	milk	130

including parathyroid and thyroid hormones, calcitonin, growth hormone, sex hormones, cortisone, and insulin. If dietary calcium is lacking, or there is a problem with absorption, the calcium bank account may become overdrawn causing problems such as tooth decay, osteoporosis, osteomalacia, and rickets.

Calcium absorption from food depends on the presence of vitamin D, and is influenced by lifestyle choices including diet, alcohol intake, smoking, and exercise. The amount absorbed depends on availability and how much is circulating in the blood.

Too much calcium in the bloodstream— usually the result of excessive calcium supplements or indigestion remedies—causes nausea, depression and even kidney stones and kidney damage. High calcium intakes are sometimes recommended for osteoporosis, but there is no firm evidence that this is effective.

Magnesium TOP 10 (milligrams per 100 grams of food)

FDA recommended intake = 420 mg/day for men; 320 mg/day for women. Toxicity level = not defined

1.	brazil nuts	410	6.	beans (on average)	110
2.	sesame seeds, sunflower seeds	380	7.	swiss chard, spinach, okra	75
3.	winkles	310	8.	anchovies, sardines, crab, prawns	50
4.	almonds, cashews, pine nuts	270	9.	cheddar cheese	39
5.	walnuts	160	10.	meat, fish (on average)	25

MAGNESIUM

Magnesium is found in most foods and after calcium is the second most abundant mineral in the body. It helps to maintain healthy bones and teeth, and protects against epilepsy, hypertension, heart disease, osteoporosis, premenstrual tension, and mental disturbance. Magnesium assists vitamin B1 in releasing energy from carbohydrates, alcohol, and fats, and vitamin B6 in the metabolism of protein. It is also needed for calcium absorption. Excess calcium in the diet reduces magnesium absorption.

It is difficult to say how much dietary magnesium is necessary because the body only absorbs what it needs at any given time, regardless of availability. If dietary magnesium is low, absorption becomes more efficient (and less is excreted by the kidneys) in order to maintain magnesium levels in the blood.

Diarrhea, diabetes, alcoholism, and diuretic drugs can all cause magnesium deficiency. Symptoms of deficiency include muscle cramps and spasms. Low intake may also be related to high blood pressure. Excess dietary magnesium may cause diarrhea, but magnesium toxicity is rare and usually only occurs in cases of kidney failure. The first signs of toxicity are thirst and flushing, followed by falling blood pressure.

Phosphorus TOP 10 (milligrams per 100 grams of food)

FDA recommended intake = 700 mg/day
Toxicity level = not defined

1.	wheat bran	1200	7.	dried beans, lentils,	
2.	yeast extract	950		chick peas	350
3.	nuts, seeds, soy beans		8.	muesli	280
	(on average)	680	9.	fish, shellfish	
4.	sardines	540		(on average)	250
5.	cheese (on average)	500	10.	eggs, meat	
6.	pearl barley, rye flour,			(on average)	200
	self-raising flour	400			

PHOSPHORUS

Phosphorus forms part of the structure of proteins, carbohydrates, and fats and is therefore present in all foods. In the body it is an important component of bones and teeth, and is also found in the chemical adenosine tri-phosphate (ATP), which is vital for the release of the energy contained in the food we eat.

A proper balance between phosphorus and calcium in the body is necessary for health. The kidneys play a central role in maintaining this balance by controlling the amount of phosphorus lost in the urine. However, it is also important to balance these two minerals in the diet. This is particularly the case with children and infants, who have smaller and more sensitive bodies than adults—too much phosphorus in a baby's diet (for example, from unprocessed cows' milk) can cause muscle spasms.

Phosphorus deficiency is very rare, but pregnancy, vitamin D deficiency, serious injury, some drugs, and alcoholism can all cause phosphorus levels to fall. This lowers immunity and may

Potassium TOP 10 (milligrams per 100 grams of food)

FDA recommended intake = 3500 mg/day

Toxicity level = 18 g/day

1.	yeast extract	2100	7.	sweet potato, avocado, greens, cabbages	450
2.	dried apricots	1880			
3.	wheat bran, wheat germ	1050	8.	banana	400
4.	beans, peas, lentils	1000	9.	potato, chicory, zucchini	360
5.	dried fruit	900	10.	meat, fish (on average)	350
6.	nuts (on average)	750			

lead to muscle weakness and softening of the bones (osteo-malacia). In children, deficiency may produce retarded growth.

POTASSIUM

Potassium boosts energy and strength, and enables nerves and muscles to function properly. It is also involved in the regulation of blood-sugar levels. Eating a diet rich in potassium helps the body to get rid of excess sodium, which in turn helps to prevent high blood pressure. Fresh fruits and vegetables contain more potassium than sodium, whereas processed fast foods and meat contain more sodium than potassium. Too much sodium in the diet (in the form of added salt) may reduce potassium levels in the body.

Potassium deficiency can be caused by gastrointestinal disorders, diabetes, diuretics, steroids, and laxatives. It produces a variety of symptoms, including poor appetite, tiredness, depression, constipation, palpitations, muscle weakness, cramps, and, in severe cases, heart failure. Potassium overload can result from excessive potassium supplements and is also caused by severe dehydration and kidney or adrenal failure. High blood levels of potassium are very toxic and lead to rapid heart failure.

SODIUM AND CHLORIDE

In nature, sodium and chloride are usually found bound together into salt, a condiment long treasured for its flavor-enhancing properties. Together with potassium, both minerals play a major role in maintaining the water balance in the body, and sodium is also important for nerve and muscle function.

Excessive sweating, burns, severe vomiting, diarrhea, diuretic therapy, and kidney damage can all cause loss of salt and water from the body. This leads to dehydration accompanied by nausea, dizziness, vomiting, muscle cramps, and exhaustion. Unless treated by the replacement of water and salt, dehydration may lead to life-threatening shock.

In affluent societies, however, excess salt causes health problems. The amount of salt needed is only a fraction of the amount routinely eaten and high blood pressure and heart disease are clearly associated with excessive salt intake.

The easiest way to reduce salt intake is to eat a diet based on fresh fruits and vegetables, and to cut down on fast foods, processed meats, and snacks. Since much of the salt we eat is incorporated into food, it is more effective to change what we eat rather than to reduce our consumption of table salt.

Sodium Chloride TOP 10 (milligrams per 100 grams of food)

WHO recommended intake = <3900 mg/day
Toxicity level = depends on individual circumstances

1.	anchovies	3930		
2.	seaweed	2500		
3.	olives	2250		
4.	bacon	1960		
5.	smoked salmon	1880		
6.	salami	1800		
7.	tomato ketchup, sweet pickle, brown sauce			1630
8.	prawns			1590
9.	feta cheese, strong blue cheese			1330
10.	pot savouries			1320

All about trace elements

IRON

The body contains iron in red blood cells, muscles, enzymes, and liver stores. It is used for transporting oxygen around the body, for hormone and bile production, for releasing energy from food, and in the elimination of toxins and waste products.

Iron exists in food in two forms—heme and non-heme. Animal-based foods contain heme iron, which is easier to absorb. Plant foods contain non-heme iron, in addition to other nutrients, such as vitamin C, which increase iron absorption. Whatever the iron content of the diet, absorption rates change according to whether body stores are depleted or full.

Worldwide, iron deficiency is a common consequence of malnutrition. In developed countries, blood loss or inhibited absorption (caused by excessive intake of tea, fiber, milk, soy, or calcium supplements) are more likely causes. Deficiency leads to anemia, causing breathlessness, palpitations, dizziness, persistent tiredness, mood changes, and poor concentration.

Iron overload, usually the result of taking supplements, causes stomach pain and constipation. Frequent iron injections,

Iron Top 10 (milligrams per 100 grams of food)

FDA recommended intake = 8 mg/day for men; 18 mg/day for women; 8 mg/day for over-50s.

Upper tolerable limit = 45 mg/day

1.	cockles	28.0	6.	fresh mint	9.5
2.	iron-fortified		7.	kidney	9.0
	breakfast cereals	24.3	8.	beans, chick peas,	
3.	wheat bran, Weetabix	12.9		lentils, wheat germ	8.3
4.	liver	11.3	9.	fresh parsley	7.7
5.	sesame seeds,		10.	dried peaches	6.8
	pumpkin seeds	10.4			

blood transfusions, various blood and liver disorders, and hemochromatosis (a hereditary disease) can also produce toxic overload, leading to heart failure and liver damage.

ZINC

Zinc is essential for growth, blood fat regulation and protein, carbohydrate, and alcohol metabolism. It promotes wound healing, the elimination of waste from working muscles, and insulin and seminal fluid production. It also protects against prostate disease and mental disturbance.

Zinc absorption is improved by vitamin B6, while excess calcium and some food additives inhibit it. Health problems such as sudden weight loss, alcohol abuse, gastrointestinal disorders, burns, and surgery cause zinc deficiency, and a typical fast food diet—high in fat and refined carbohydrate—is low in zinc.

Symptoms of deficiency include loss of appetite, diarrhea, skin problems, poor wound healing, lowered immunity, loss of taste and smell, hair loss, white spots on the nails, tiredness, mental disturbance, and "pica" (eating dirt) in children. Too much zinc, usually from supplements, causes nausea and vomiting, and may interfere with copper, iron, and calcium absorption.

Zinc TOP 10 (milligrams per 100 grams of food)

FDA recommended intake = 11 mg/day for men; 8 mg/day for women. Toxicity level = 2 g in a single dose; 50 mg/day, long-term.

1.	wheat germ, bran	17.0	7.	cod roe	3.3
2.	liver	15.9	8.	wholewheat pasta,	
3.	whelks	12.1		beans, chick peas	3.0
4.	nuts, seeds	5.3	9.	anchovies, sardines,	
5.	soy beans, lentils	4.0		shellfish	2.5
6.	kidney, meat,		10.	oatcakes	2.3
	cheese	3.5			

MANGANESE

Manganese is vital for healthy bones. It is also involved in protein, fat, and cholesterol metabolism, preserving cell membranes and preventing heart disease, cancer, rheumatoid arthritis, diabetes, and epilepsy.

Severe deficiency is virtually unknown, but absorption from the gut is inhibited by the presence of calcium, phosphorus, and zinc. Mild deficiency has been linked with cancer, myasthenia gravis, rheumatoid arthritis, diabetes, atherosclerosis, heart disease, epilepsy, and schizophrenia. Excess manganese—from

Manganese TOP 10 (milligrams per 100 grams of food)

Upper tolerable limit = 11 mg/day

1.	dried sage	25.0	8.	muesli, chick peas,
2.	wheat germ	12.3		soy beans 2.6
3.	wheat bran	9.0	9.	peanuts, coconut,
4.	pine nuts	7.9		cashews, almonds,
5.	macadamia nuts,			sunflower seeds,
	hazelnuts, pecans	5.2		sesame seeds 2.0
6.	oyster mushrooms	3.6	10.	blackberries, lentils,
7.	walnuts	3.4		tempeh, tofu 1.3

taking supplements or in drinking water—may cause psychosis and a neurological condition resembling Parkinson's disease.

COPPER

Copper helps to keep red blood cells healthy and may protect against osteoporosis and arthritis. Deficiency is uncommon but occurs in cases of malnutrition, malabsorption, and chronic diarrhea. Zinc, cadmium, fluoride, and molybdenum supplements may inhibit absorption. Symptoms of deficiency include anemia, osteoporosis, lowered immunity, de-pigmentation, poor growth, and hypothyroidism.

Copper TOP 10 (milligrams per 100 grams of food)

FDA recommended intake = 0.9 mg/day
Toxicity level = uncertain

1.	calf liver	23.86	6.	cashew nuts	2.11
2.	lamb liver	13.54	7.	brazil nuts	1.76
3.	whelks	6.59	8.	winkles	1.70
4.	beef liver, pig liver	2.40	9.	soy beans, crab,	
5.	sunflower seeds,			lobster	1.50
	melon seeds	2.30	10.	sesame seeds,	
				pumpkin seeds	1.48

Iodine TOP 10 (micrograms per 100 grams of food)

FDA recommended intake = 150 µg/day

Toxicity level = 1000 µg/day

1.	dried seaweed,		6.	– , nori	1470
	kombu	448670	7.	cockles, mussels	140
2.	– , arame	84140	8.	cod, lobster	100
3.	– , hijiki	42670	9.	kipper, yogurt, eggs	63
4.	– , wakame	16830	10.	salmon, butter, milk,	
5.	– , dulse	5970		cheese	31

iodized salt contains 3100 µg

sea salt contains 50 µg

IODINE

Iodine is a vital component of the thyroid hormones that regulate metabolism and tissue repair, and promote growth and development. Iodine deficiency is uncommon in developed countries but is a problem in developing parts of the world causing goitre (enlarged thyroid) and thyroid underactivity. This results in weight gain, lethargy, constipation, dry skin and hair, and (sometimes) mental disturbance. Iodine deficiency may also cause retarded growth and impaired mental development in children. A high intake of iodine causes thyroid dysfunction.

SELENIUM

Selenium is an antioxidant, which boosts immunity and helps red blood cells to function properly. The amount of selenium in plants depends on how much they absorb from the soil so the amount of selenium in food is very variable. Pollution and intensive farming have reduced soil selenium levels and food processing methods also reduce the selenium content in food.

Deficiency lowers immunity and is linked with cancer, heart disease, stroke, eye disease, and male infertility. Severe deficiency in young people causes degenerative heart disease. Supplement overdose may cause hair loss, brittle nails, itchy skin rash, and, in severe cases, neurological disturbance and paralysis.

Selenium TOP 10 (micrograms per 100 grams of food)

FDA recommended intake = 55 µg/day
Upper tolerable limit = 400 µg/day

1.	brazil nuts	254	7.	sunflower seeds	49
2.	kidney	209	8.	mussels	43
3.	lentils	105	9.	sardines, plaice,	
4.	tuna	78		kipper, mackerel	39
5.	squid, sole, lobster	62	10.	cashew nuts	34
6.	liver	50			

MINERAL AND TRACE ELEMENT TABLES

These tables give the calorie, mineral, and trace element contents of a wide selection of foods. The minerals listed are calcium, magnesium, phosphorus, potassium, and sodium chloride. The trace elements are iron, zinc, manganese, copper, iodine, and selenium. The calorie, mineral, and trace element contents of each food are given "per average portion" rather than weight for weight. This allows you to work out the nutrient content of your diet without using weights or measures.

To find out how rich a food is in a particular mineral or trace element, compare the amount contained in a single portion ("n" is given where the figure is not known; "tr" denotes trace) with the Quality Calorie Target (QCT) given at the top of the column. This will enable you to assess your daily intake, and help you choose foods that will boost your intake of particular minerals and trace elements. The figures in bold denote the foods with the highest nutrient scores in each food category.

FRUIT

FOOD	AVERAGE PORTION SIZE	TOTAL CALORIES	MINERALS	
(where appropriate, numbers in brackets represent number of fruit in average portion)	oz per portion	kcals per portion	Calcium (mg/portion) (QCT: 1000mg/day)	Magnesium (mg/portion) (QCT: 320mg/day)
Fresh fruit				
Apple (1)	3 ½	47	4	5
Apricot (2)	4 ½	40	20	14
Date (4)	3 ½	124	24	24
Fig (2)	4	47	42	17
Grapes (bunch)	3 ½	60	13	7
Kiwi fruit (2)	4	59	30	18
Melon (all types) (1 slice)	6 ½	43	25	20
Peach/nectarine (1)	5	55	11	15
Pear (1)	6	68	19	12
Persimmon (1)	4	80	11	12
Plum/greengage (2)	3 ½	39	17	8
Rhubarb	3 ½	7	93	13
Tropical fruit				
Banana (1)	3 ½	95	6	34
Guava (1)	5	36	18	17
Lychee (5)	2 ½	44	5	7
Mango (½)	6 ½	103	22	23
Papaya/paw-paw (¼)	5	50	32	15
Passionfruit (5)	2 ½	27	8	22
Pineapple (2 slices)	5 ½	66	29	26
Pomegranate (1)	3 ½	51	12	11
Citrus fruit				
Clementine/satsuma/tangerine (2)	4	43	37	12
Grapefruit/pomelo (1)	6 ½	54	41	16
Lemon/lime (1)	3 ½	12	25	10
Orange (1)	5 ½	59	75	16
Berries				
Blackberries (20)	3 ½	25	41	23
Blackcurrants	3 ½	28	60	17

continues

	MINERALS				TRACE ELEMENTS			
Phosphorus (mg/portion) (QCI: 700mg/day)	Potassium (mg/portion) (QCI: 3500mg/day)	Sodium Chloride (mg/portion) (max: 3900mg/day)	Copper (mg/portion) (QCI: 0.9mg/day)	Iron (mg/portion) (QCI: 18mg/day)	Iodine (µg/portion) (QCI: 150µg/day)	Manganese (mg/portion) (QCI: 1.8mg/day)	Selenium (µg/portion) (QCI: 55µg/day)	Zinc (mg/portion) (QCI: 8mg/day)
11	120	3	0.02	0.1	tr	0.1	tr	0.1
26	351	3	0.08	0.7	tr	0.1	1	0.1
28	410	7	0.12	0.3	n	0.2	1	0.2
17	220	3	0.07	0.3	n	0.1	tr	0.3
18	210	2	0.12	0.3	1	0.1	1	0.1
38	348	5	0.16	0.5	n	0.1	n	0.1
23	342	43	tr	0.4	n	tr	tr	tr
33	255	2	0.09	0.6	5	0.2	tr	0.2
22	255	5	0.10	0.3	2	tr	tr	0.2
21	231	6	0.11	0.1	n	0.3	n	0.1
23	310	2	0.10	0.4	tr	0.1	tr	0.1
17	290	3	0.07	0.3	n	0.2	tr	0.1
28	400	1	0.10	0.3	8	0.4	1	0.2
35	322	7	0.14	0.6	n	0.1	n	0.3
23	120	1	0.11	0.4	n	0.1	n	0.2
29	324	4	0.22	1.3	n	0.5	n	0.2
18	280	7	0.11	0.7	n	0.1	n	0.3
48	158	14	n	1.0	n	n	n	0.6
16	256	3	0.18	0.3	tr	0.8	tr	0.2
29	240	2	0.17	0.7	n	n	n	0.4
22	156	5	0.01	0.1	n	tr	n	0.1
36	360	5	0.04	0.2	n	tr	2	tr
18	130	2	0.05	0.4	n	tr	n	0.1
34	240	8	0.08	0.2	3	tr	2	0.2
31	160	2	0.11	0.7	n	1.4	tr	0.2
43	120	3	0.14	1.3	n	0.3	n	0.3

FRUIT

FOOD	AVERAGE PORTION SIZE	TOTAL CALORIES	MINERALS	
(where appropriate, numbers in brackets represent number of fruit in average portion)	oz per portion	kcals per portion	Calcium (mg/portion) (QCT: 1000mg/day)	Magnesium (mg/portion) (QCT: 320mg/day)
Blueberries (bilberries)	3 ½	30	12	5
Cherries (10)	3 ½	48	13	10
Cranberries	3 ½	15	12	7
Elderberries	3 ½	35	37	n
Gooseberries	3 ½	40	19	9
Raspberries (25)	3 ½	25	25	19
Redcurrants	3 ½	21	36	13
Strawberries (10)	4	32	19	12
Dried fruit				
Apricot (10)	3 ½	132	92	65
Date (6)	3 ½	203	45	41
Fig (5)	3 ½	227	**250**	80
Pear (10 slices)	3 ½	207	55	35
Pineapple (6 slices)	3 ½	276	120	**110**
Prune (10)	3 ½	160	38	27
Raisins (3 tbs)	3 ½	163	46	35

| | MINERALS | | | TRACE ELEMENTS | | | | | |
Phosphoros (mg/portion) (QCT: 700mg/day)	Potassium (mg/portion) (QCT: 3500mg/day)	Sodium Chloride (mg/portion) (max: 3900mg/day)	Copper (mg/portion) (QCT: 0.9mg/day)	Iron (mg/portion) (QCT: 18mg/day)	Iodine (µg/portion) (QCT: 150µg/day)	Manganese (mg/portion) (QCT: 1.8mg/day)	Selenium (µg/portion) (QCT: 55µg/day)	Zinc (mg/portion) (QCT: 8mg/day)
14	88	3	0.08	0.5	n	0.3	tr	0.2
21	210	1	0.07	0.2	tr	0.1	1	0.1
11	95	2	0.05	0.7	n	0.1	n	0.2
48	290	1	n	1.6	n	n	n	n
19	170	1	0.06	0.6	tr	0.1	tr	0.1
31	170	3	0.10	0.7	n	0.4	n	0.3
30	280	2	0.12	1.2	n	0.2	n	0.2
29	192	7	0.08	0.5	11	0.4	tr	0.1
120	**1,880**	56	0.40	4.1	n	0.4	7	**0.7**
60	700	10	0.26	1.3	n	0.3	3	0.4
89	970	**62**	0.30	**4.2**	n	0.5	tr	0.7
65	750	15	0.30	1.0	5	0.2	2	0.5
65	1,080	15	**0.74**	1.3	tr	**3.4**	tr	**0.7**
83	860	12	0.16	2.9	n	0.3	3	0.5
76	1,020	60	0.39	3.8	n	0.3	**8**	**0.7**

NUTS AND SEEDS

FOOD	AVERAGE PORTION SIZE	TOTAL CALORIES	MINERALS	
	oz per portion	kcals per portion	Calcium (mg/portion) (QCT: 1000mg/day)	Magnesium (mg/portion) (QCT: 320mg/day)
Almonds	1 ¾	306	120	135
Brazil nuts	1 ¾	341	85	205
Cashew nuts	1 ¾	287	16	135
Chestnuts, dried	1 ¾	160	10	6
Coconut, fresh	3 ½	351	13	41
Coconut, desiccated	1 ¾	302	12	45
Hazelnuts	1 ¾	325	70	80
Macadamia nuts (salted)	1 ¾	374	24	50
Melon seeds	1 ¾	292	36	255
Peanuts	1 ¾	282	30	105
Peanut butter	¾	125	7	36
Pecan nuts	1 ¾	345	31	65
Pine nuts	1 ¾	344	6	135
Pistachio nuts (salted)	1 ¾	301	55	65
Pumpkin seeds	1 ¾	285	20	135
Sesame seeds	1 ¾	299	335	185
Sesame spread (tahini)	1 ¾	304	340	190
Sunflower seeds	1 ¾	291	55	195
Walnuts	1 ¾	344	47	80

	MINERALS					TRACE ELEMENTS		
Phosphorus (mg/portion) (QCT: 700mg/day)	Potassium (mg/portion) (QCT: 3500mg/day)	Sodium Chloride (mg/portion) (max: 3900mg/day)	Copper (mg/portion) (QCT: 0.9mg/day)	Iron (mg/portion) (QCT: 18mg/day)	Iodine (µg/portion) (QCT: 150µg/day)	Manganese (mg/portion) (QCT: 1.8mg/day)	Selenium (µg/portion) (QCT: 55µg/day)	Zinc (mg/portion) (QCT: 8mg/day)
275	390	7	0.50	1.5	1	0.9	2	1.6
295	330	2	0.88	1.3	**10**	0.6	**765**	2.1
280	355	8	1.06	3.1	6	0.9	15	3.0
26	190	33	0.01	0.5	3	0.4	1	0.2
94	370	17	0.32	2.1	1	1.0	3	0.5
80	330	14	0.28	1.8	2	0.9	2	0.5
150	365	3	0.62	1.6	9	2.5	tr	1.1
100	150	140	0.22	0.8	n	2.8	4	0.6
345	325	50	**1.20**	3.8	n	1.2	n	2.0
215	335	1	0.51	1.3	**10**	1.1	2	1.8
66	140	70	0.14	0.4	n	0.3	1	0.6
155	260	1	0.54	1.1	n	2.3	6	2.7
325	390	1	0.66	2.8	n	**4.0**	n	**3.3**
210	**520**	**265**	0.42	1.5	n	0.5	3	3.0
425	410	9	0.79	5.0	n	n	n	**3.3**
360	285	10	0.73	5.2	n	0.8	n	2.7
365	290	10	0.74	**5.3**	n	0.8	n	2.7
320	355	2	1.14	3.2	n	1.1	25	2.6
190	225	4	0.67	1.5	5	1.7	10	1.4

VEGETABLES AND PULSES

FOOD	AVERAGE PORTION SIZE	TOTAL CALORIES	MINERALS	
	oz per portion	kcals per portion	Calcium (mg/portion) (QCT: 1000mg/day)	Magnesium (mg/portion) (QCT: 320mg/day)
Root vegetables				
Beet	3 ½	36	20	11
Carrot	3 ½	35	25	3
Celeriac	3 ½	18	40	21
Parsnip	3 ½	64	41	23
Potato, baked	6 ½	245	20	58
Potato, boiled in salted water	6 ½	130	9	25
Potato, mashed	6 ½	187	22	23
Potato, fries (all types, average)	6 ½	398	20	45
Rutabaga	3 ½	24	53	9
Sweet potato, baked	4 ½	150	40	30
Beans, peas, and lentils				
Aduki beans, cooked	3 ½	123	39	60
Baked beans, in tomato sauce	4 ½	105	62	40
Bean sprouts, fresh	2	19	12	11
Blackeye/pigeon/mung beans (av.)	3 ½	99	21	45
Chick peas, cooked	3 ½	121	46	37
Fava beans, fresh	4	71	28	29
Green beans (haricot verts), fresh	3 ½	24	36	17
Haricot beans, dried, cooked	3 ½	95	65	45
Lentils, cooked (all types, average)	3 ½	105	22	34
Lima beans, cooked	3 ½	103	19	38
Peas, fresh	3 ½	83	21	34
Pinto beans, cooked	3 ½	137	47	56
Red kidney beans, cooked	3 ½	103	37	45
String beans, yard-long, fresh	3 ½	22	33	19
Soy beans, black, cooked	3 ½	141	83	63
Tempeh (fermented soybean)	3 ½	166	120	70
Tofu (soybean curd)	3 ½	73	**1,480**	67

continues

	MINERALS							TRACE ELEMENTS	
Phosphorus (mg/portion) (QCT: 700mg/day)	Potassium (mg/portion) (QCT: 3500mg/day)	Sodium Chloride (mg/portion) (max: 3900mg/day)	Copper (mg/portion) (QCT: 0.9mg/day)	Iron (mg/portion) (QCT: 18mg/day)	Iodine (µg/portion) (QCT: 150µg/day)	Manganese (mg/portion) (QCT: 1.8mg/day)	Selenium (µg/portion) (QCT: 55µg/day)	Zinc (mg/portion) (QCT: 8mg/day)
51	380	66	0.02	1.0	n	0.7	tr	0.4
15	170	25	0.02	0.3	2	0.1	1	0.1
63	460	91	0.04	0.8	n	0.1	n	0.3
74	450	10	0.05	0.6	n	0.5	2	0.3
122	1,134	22	0.25	1.3	9	0.4	4	0.9
56	504	121	0.13	0.7	5	0.2	5	0.5
61	468	88	0.11	0.7	9	0.2	2	0.5
112	**1,188**	558	0.25	1.4	9	0.4	4	1.1
40	170	15	0.01	0.1	n	0.1	1	0.3
85	624	68	0.23	1.2	4	0.7	1	0.5
180	570	2	0.51	1.9	n	0.8	2	2.3
124	390	**715**	0.05	1.8	4	0.4	3	0.7
29	44	3	0.05	1.0	n	0.2	n	0.2
140	320	5	0.22	1.9	n	0.5	3	1.1
83	270	5	0.28	2.1	n	0.7	1	1.2
156	372	1	0.13	1.1	5	0.2	n	1.1
38	230	tr	0.01	1.2	n	n	n	0.2
120	320	15	0.14	2.5	n	0.7	4	1.0
130	310	3	0.33	3.5	n	0.5	**40**	1.4
87	400	9	0.16	1.7	n	0.5	n	0.9
130	330	1	0.05	2.8	2	0.4	1	1.1
150	460	1	0.26	2.3	n	0.5	6	1.0
130	420	2	0.23	2.5	n	0.5	6	1.0
34	34	tr	0.02	1.2	2	0.2	n	0.2
250	510	1	0.32	3.0	2	0.7	5	0.9
200	370	6	0.67	**3.6**	n	**1.4**	n	1.8
270	180	12	0.58	3.5	n	1.2	n	2.0

VEGETABLES AND PULSES

FOOD	AVERAGE PORTION SIZE	TOTAL CALORIES	MINERALS	
(where appropriate, numbers in brackets represent number of vegetables in average portion)	oz per portion	kcals per portion	Calcium (mg/portion) (QCT: 1000mg/day)	Magnesium (mg/portion) (QCT: 320mg/day)
Miscellaneous vegetables				
Artichoke hearts (2)	3 ½	18	41	23
Asparagus (5 spears)	4 ½	31	38	16
Avocado (1)	5	276	16	36
Beet greens	3 ½	33	210	19
Broccoli, green/purple	3 ½	34	128	23
Brussels sprouts (9)	3 ½	42	26	8
Cabbage (all types, average)	3 ½	26	52	8
Cauliflower	3 ½	34	21	17
Celery (3 sticks)	3 ½	7	41	5
Chicory	3 ½	13	44	10
Cucumber (2 in chunk)	4	12	22	10
Curly kale	3 ½	33	130	34
Eggplant (½)	4 ½	20	13	14
Fennel	3 ½	12	24	8
Lettuce (all types, average)	2 ¾	10	32	6
Mushrooms, common	3 ½	13	6	9
Mushrooms, shiitake	1 ¾	28	tr	7
Okra (gumbo)	3 ½	31	160	71
Olive (10)	1	31	18	7
Onion/leek (all types, average)	3 ½	28	25	6
Pepper, green/red (½)	2 ¾	19	6	10
Pumpkin	6 ½	23	52	18
Seaweed, dried (all types, av.)	½	8	66	36
Spinach	3 ½	25	170	54
Sweetcorn	3 ½	93	3	37
Swiss chard	3 ½	19	51	**81**
Tomato (1)	3	14	6	6
Watercress	3	18	136	12
Zucchini	3 ½	18	25	22

	MINERALS				TRACE ELEMENTS			
Phosphorus (mg/portion) (QCT: 700mg/day)	Potassium (mg/portion) (QCT: 3500mg/day)	Sodium Chloride (mg/portion) (max: 3900mg/day)	Copper (mg/portion) (QCT: 0.9mg/day)	Iron (mg/portion) (QCT: 18mg/day)	Iodine (µg/portion) (QCT: 150µg/day)	Manganese (mg/portion) (QCT: 1.8mg/day)	Selenium (µg/portion) (QCT: 55µg/day)	Zinc (mg/portion) (QCT: 8mg/day)
38	360	27	0.09	0.7	n	0.3	tr	0.5
90	325	1	0.10	0.5	tr	0.3	1	0.9
57	653	9	0.28	0.6	3	0.3	tr	0.6
91	370	20	0.02	3.0	n	n	n	0.4
72	375	9	0.02	1.8	2	0.2	tr	0.6
77	450	6	0.02	0.7	1	0.2	n	0.5
41	270	6	0.02	0.2	2	0.2	1	0.3
64	380	9	0.03	0.7	tr	0.3	tr	0.6
21	320	60	0.02	0.4	n	0.1	3	0.1
67	380	10	0.01	2.8	n	0.3	1	0.2
59	168	4	0.01	0.4	4	0.1	tr	0.1
61	450	43	0.03	1.7	2	0.8	2	0.4
21	273	3	0.01	0.4	1	0.1	1	0.3
26	440	11	0.02	0.3	n	n	n	0.5
28	232	3	0.02	0.9	2	0.2	1	0.2
80	320	5	**0.72**	0.6	3	0.1	9	0.4
15	60	2	n	n	n	n	n	n
59	330	8	0.13	1.1	n	n	1	0.6
5	27	675	0.07	0.3	n	tr	n	n
37	620	4	0.05	1.0	3	0.1	1	0.5
17	112	3	0.02	0.3	1	0.1	tr	0.1
34	234	tr	0.04	0.7	n	0.2	n	0.4
29	117	193	0.12	1.5	**1,683**	0.6	1	**51.0**
45	500	140	0.04	2.1	2	0.6	1	0.7
91	260	1	0.04	0.7	n	0.2	tr	0.4
46	380	210	n	1.8	n	n	n	n
20	213	8	0.09	0.4	2	0.1	tr	0.1
42	184	39	0.01	1.8	n	0.5	n	0.6
45	360	1	0.02	0.8	n	0.1	1	0.3

VEGETABLE DISHES

FOOD	AVERAGE PORTION SIZE	TOTAL CALORIES	MINERALS	
(where appropriate, numbers in brackets represent number of items in average portion)	oz per portion	kcals per portion	Calcium (mg/portion) (QCT: 1000mg/day)	Magnesium (mg/portion) (QCT: 320mg/day)
Bakes and flans				
Cannelloni	7	**290**	208	28
Casserole, bean and vegetable	9	**115**	58	40
Cauliflower cheese	7	**210**	240	36
Cottage pie, vegetable	10	**339**	36	42
Flan, vegetable	4	**253**	145	14
Lasagne, vegetable	16	**527**	329	81
Moussaka, vegetable	12	**480**	266	88
Nut roast	5	**528**	116	**170**
Pizza, cheese and tomato	10	**711**	**630**	57
Burgers, cutlets, and pancakes				
Beanburger (no bun)	2 ½	**152**	52	39
Dosa with vegetable filling (1)	7	**307**	48	64
Falafel (3)	3 ½	**179**	80	45
Nut cutlet (2)	4	**347**	101	72
Onion bhaji/pakora (1)	1 ¾	**156**	49	31
Pancake with vegetable filling (1)	7	**298**	160	26
Quorn (myco-protein)	3 ½	**86**	28	31
Samosa, vegetable (1)	3 ½	**217**	65	19
Tempeh burger (1)	2	**116**	25	27
Tofu burger (1)	2	**71**	198	26
Vegeburger (1)	2	**147**	54	41
Curries, stews, and rice dishes				
Bhaji, cauliflower	9	**535**	68	55
Bhaji, mushroom	9	**415**	45	20
Bhaji, potato	9	**395**	48	60
Broccoli in cheese sauce	7	**236**	320	32
Colcannon (fried)	7	**248**	38	18
Curry, cauliflower and potato	9	**148**	53	50
Curry, chick pea and spinach	9	**498**	213	108

continues

	MINERALS			TRACE ELEMENTS				
Phosphorus (mg/portion) (QCT: 700mg/day)	Potassium (mg/portion) (QCT: 3500mg/day)	Sodium Chloride (mg/portion) (max: 3900mg/day)	Copper (mg/portion) (QCT: 0.9mg/day)	Iron (mg/portion) (QCT: 18mg/day)	Iodine (µg/portion) (QCT: 150µg/day)	Manganese (mg/portion) (QCT: 1.8mg/day)	Selenium (µg/portion) (QCT: 55µg/day)	Zinc (mg/portion) (QCT: 8mg/day)
186	234	532	0.10	1.0	n	0.4	n	1.2
128	795	322	0.15	1.5	8	0.5	3	0.8
238	618	398	0.06	1.2	22	0.4	2	1.8
108	720	1,020	0.21	1.8	n	0.3	**21**	0.9
110	149	322	0.06	1.0	n	0.2	1	0.7
392	855	**1,755**	0.09	3.6	n	0.9	n	1.8
350	**1,155**	1,575	0.21	3.5	n	0.7	n	1.8
392	632	510	0.81	3.2	14	**2.1**	6	3.0
480	480	1740	0.36	3.3	**39**	0.9	12	2.4
135	360	165	0.29	1.6	n	0.5	2	1.4
149	600	850	0.32	3.1	8	0.5	2	1.4
130	380	290	0.29	2.8	n	0.5	1	1.0
168	228	252	0.38	1.6	n	0.4	n	1.2
85	275	110	0.16	2.1	2	0.4	1	0.8
166	460	300	0.24	1.6	28	0.3	6	0.8
220	120	310	0.81	0.4	n	**2.1**	n	**7.5**
65	150	390	0.11	1.5	n	0.2	n	0.5
84	108	78	0.23	0.8	n	0.4	n	0.6
102	108	126	0.14	1.1	n	0.6	n	1.0
126	318	252	0.21	2.1	n	0.4	4	0.8
183	1,075	1,050	0.10	2.3	8	0.5	tr	1.8
155	700	n	1.08	1.8	13	0.2	13	1.0
113	975	950	0.25	2.8	13	0.4	3	1.0
260	340	460	0.04	1.4	26	0.1	4	1.4
56	400	14	0.08	0.8	8	0.3	4	0.4
155	1,025	525	0.15	2.0	3	0.5	tr	1.5
218	800	108	0.63	**5.8**	n	1.4	3	2.3

VEGETABLE DISHES

FOOD	AVERAGE PORTION SIZE	TOTAL CALORIES	MINERALS	
(where appropriate, numbers in brackets represent number of items in average portion)	oz per portion	kcals per portion	Calcium (mg/portion) (QCT: 1000mg/day)	Magnesium (mg/portion) (QCT: 320mg/day)
Curry, red lentil and mung bean	9	285	38	58
Curry, red lentil and tomato	9	230	43	40
Curry, okra	9	273	300	133
Curry, mixed vegetable	9	123	48	28
Okra with tomato and onion	9	450	375	165
Ratatouille	9	205	43	38
Risotto (brown rice)	12	501	88	140
Side dishes, dips, spreads, and sauces				
Guacamole	3 ¹/₂	128	9	19
Houmous	2	112	25	37
Pesto sauce	1	129	140	17
Red cabbage, stewed with apple	3 ¹/₂	59	46	8
Tofu spread	1 ³/₄	104	125	9
Vegetable pâté	1 ³/₄	87	65	14
Vegetable stir-fry	3 ¹/₂	64	30	16
Vine leaves, stuffed with rice (3)	3 ¹/₂	262	130	24
Salads				
Coleslaw, with vinaigrette	3 ¹/₂	87	37	35
Salad, bean, with vinaigrette	3 ¹/₂	147	36	24
Salad, beet, with vinaigrette	3 ¹/₂	100	26	14
Salad, carrot, nut, with vinaigrette	3 ¹/₂	218	38	23
Salad, Greek	3 ¹/₂	130	61	9
Salad, green (no dressing)	3 ¹/₂	12	19	7
Salad, pasta, veg., w. mayonnaise	3 ¹/₂	127	14	11
Salad, potato, with vinaigrette	3 ¹/₂	157	9	13
Salad, potato, with mayonnaise	3 ¹/₂	239	8	10
Salad, Waldorf	3 ¹/₂	193	13	12
Tabouleh/couscous salad	3 ¹/₂	119	27	33

	MINERALS				TRACE ELEMENTS			
Phosphorus (mg/portion) (QCI: 700mg/day)	Potassium (mg/portion) (QCI: 3500mg/day)	Sodium Chloride (mg/portion) (max: 3900mg/day)	Copper (mg/portion) (QCI: 0.9mg/day)	Iron (mg/portion) (QCI: 18mg/day)	Iodine (µg/portion) (QCI: 150µg/day)	Manganese (mg/portion) (QCI: 1.8mg/day)	Selenium (µg/portion) (QCI: 55µg/day)	Zinc (mg/portion) (QCI: 8mg/day)
175	525	525	0.23	4.0	n	n	5	1.5
135	600	525	0.23	3.8	n	n	3	1.3
138	875	750	0.30	2.5	n	n	3	1.3
68	475	53	0.13	2.0	5	0.4	tr	0.5
160	975	325	0.33	3.0	n	n	3	1.5
78	700	500	0.05	1.3	n	0.2	3	0.5
455	910	1,155	**1.30**	4.2	n	1.3	18	2.8
32	370	140	0.13	0.4	2	0.1	tr	0.3
96	114	402	0.18	1.1	n	0.3	n	0.8
120	63	120	0.10	0.6	n	0.3	n	0.9
31	210	32	0.02	0.4	2	0.1	2	0.1
33	60	345	0.06	0.5	n	0.1	n	0.2
95	150	270	0.07	2.1	n	0.2	n	1.1
46	230	11	0.11	0.5	n	0.1	tr	0.3
53	190	1,140	0.56	1.1	4	0.3	2	0.5
24	190	130	0.02	0.4	2	0.1	3	0.2
74	190	280	0.07	1.5	n	0.2	2	0.5
72	420	150	0.03	0.7	n	0.5	tr	0.4
50	300	130	0.18	0.8	3	0.4	1	0.3
61	150	360	0.03	0.4	n	0.1	n	0.2
33	160	6	0.01	0.4	2	0.1	tr	0.1
37	84	51	0.06	0.6	4	0.1	tr	0.4
28	240	120	0.06	0.5	3	0.1	1	0.3
30	210	130	0.05	0.4	12	0.1	n	0.2
35	130	88	0.10	0.3	7	0.2	n	0.3
79	140	76	n	1.8	n	n	n	n

MEAT AND MEAT DISHES

FOOD	AVERAGE PORTION SIZE	TOTAL CALORIES	MINERALS	
	oz per portion	kcals per portion	Calcium (mg/portion) (QCT: 1000mg/day)	Magnesium (mg/portion) (QCT: 320mg/day)
Beef				
Ground	7	458	36	40
Roast	4	341	12	23
Steak	4	295	8	29
Veal cutlet	5	323	15	50
Lamb				
Chop	5 ½	443	11	30
Cutlet	3 ½	244	6	15
Roast	4	319	10	30
Pork				
Bacon	3 ½	477	13	20
Chop	4	395	10	20
Roast	4	343	12	26
Poultry and game				
Chicken, roast	4	259	11	25
Duck, roast	4	407	14	19
Goose, roast	4	383	12	37
Grouse, roast	4	208	36	49
Pheasant, roast	4	256	59	42
Rabbit, roast or stewed	4	230	19	26
Squab, roast	4	276	19	43
Turkey, roast	4	205	11	29
Venison, roast or stewed	4	238	13	26
Variety meats				
Heart (all types, average)	3 ½	208	6	22
Kidney (all types, average)	3 ½	160	9	17
Liver (all types, average)	3 ½	213	7	20
Oxtail	3 ½	243	14	18
Tripe	5	150	90	26

continues

	MINERALS				TRACE ELEMENTS			
Phosphorus (mg/portion) (QCT: 700mg/day)	Potassium (mg/portion) (QCT: 3500mg/day)	Sodium Chloride (mg/portion) (max: 3900mg/day)	Copper (mg/portion) (QCT: 0.9mg/day)	Iron (mg/portion) (QCT: 18mg/day)	Iodine (µg/portion) (QCT: 150µg/day)	Manganese (mg/portion) (QCT: 1.8mg/day)	Selenium (µg/portion) (QCT: 55µg/day)	Zinc (mg/portion) (QCT: 8mg/day)
340	580	640	0.48	6.2	18	tr	14	**7.8**
204	360	65	0.22	2.3	11	tr	8	4.2
264	432	65	0.18	3.8	13	tr	8	4.2
420	630	165	n	2.0	14	tr	14	4.7
256	400	90	0.21	2.4	11	tr	5	3.2
130	210	47	0.12	1.3	8	tr	3	1.9
240	372	78	0.34	3.0	7	tr	5	6.1
170	300	1,870	0.12	1.3	7	tr	7	1.5
192	348	67	0.16	1.0	10	tr	13	1.6
240	420	95	0.30	1.6	4	tr	24	3.5
204	324	86	0.14	1.0	7	tr	20	2.6
180	252	91	0.32	3.2	n	tr	26	3.1
324	492	180	0.59	5.5	n	tr	n	3.1
408	564	115	n	9.1	n	n	n	n
372	492	120	n	10.1	n	tr	17	1.6
270	252	43	n	7.6	n	n	19	2.0
480	492	132	n	**23.3**	n	n	n	n
240	336	62	0.17	1.1	10	tr	20	3.0
348	432	103	n	9.4	n	tr	17	4.7
220	300	105	0.47	4.4	n	tr	n	2.8
250	260	200	0.55	6.0	n	tr	**209**	3.6
350	310	84	**5.08**	11.0	n	0.5	62	5.2
140	170	190	0.27	3.8	n	n	n	8.8
65	180	5	0.21	2.0	n	n	n	n

MEAT AND MEAT DISHES

FOOD (where appropriate, numbers in brackets represent number of items in average portion)	AVERAGE PORTION SIZE oz per portion	TOTAL CALORIES kcals per portion	MINERALS Calcium (mg/portion) (QCI: 1000mg/day)	Magnesium (mg/portion) (QCI: 320mg/day)
Cold meats				
Corned beef	1	54	4	4
Ham	1	30	tr	5
Processed meat	1	78	4	2
Tongue (pressed)	1	53	8	4
Burgers and sausages				
Beefburger, quarterpounder	2 ¾	211	26	18
Liver sausage (1)	1 ¾	155	13	6
Salami (2 slices)	1	167	3	3
Sausage (all types, average) (1)	1 ¾	157	21	6
Turkey burger/escalope	3 ¼	119	6	26
Meat dishes				
Black pudding	2 ½	229	26	12
Bolognese sauce	7 ¾	306	57	40
Chicken chow mein	12	515	161	39
Cornish pasty	5 ½	515	93	28
Cottage pie	10	357	45	48
Haggis	3 ½	310	29	36
Hot pot	11 ½	376	73	83
Irish stew	11 ½	409	40	59
Lamb curry	11 ½	528	109	73
Lasagne	12	669	350	67
Moussaka	11 ½	644	290	69
Pork pie	5	564	71	24
Samosa (lamb)	3 ½	578	35	13
Sausage roll	2	287	42	8
Shish kebab (in pita with salad)	9 ½	419	92	51
Spring roll	3 ½	242	32	13
Steak and kidney pie	7	646	106	36
Tandoori chicken	12	749	203	126

	MINERALS			TRACE ELEMENTS					
Phosphorus (mg/portion) (QCT: 700mg/day)	Potassium (mg/portion) (QCT: 3500mg/day)	Sodium Chloride (mg/portion) (max: 3900mg/day)	Copper (mg/portion) (QCT: 0.9mg/day)	Iron (mg/portion) (QCT: 18mg/day)	Iodine (µg/portion) (QCT: 150µg/day)	Manganese (mg/portion) (QCT: 1.8mg/day)	Selenium (µg/portion) (QCT: 55µg/day)	Zinc (mg/portion) (QCT: 8mg/day)	
30	35	238	0.06	0.7	4	tr	2	1.4	
70	70	313	0.06	0.3	1	tr	3	0.5	
50	35	263	0.08	0.3	n	tr	2	0.4	
35	24	263	0.07	0.6	n	n	n	n	
200	272	704	0.20	2.0	5	tr	8	5.0	
115	85	430	0.32	3.2	n	0.1	n	1.2	
54	54	629	0.08	0.3	5	tr	2	1.0	
73	68	425	0.13	0.7	4	0.1	3	0.7	
207	306	41	0.13	0.5	n	n	n	1.4	
83	105	908	0.28	15.0	n	n	n	1.0	
178	682	968	0.31	3.5	15	0.2	9	5.1	
224	315	1,631	0.18	3.5	n	0.4	n	0.1	
171	295	915	0.54	2.3	5	0.3	3	0.9	
207	720	1,350	0.39	3.3	n	n	n	5.7	
160	170	770	0.44	4.8	n	n	n	1.9	
274	1,419	**2,211**	0.53	4.0	n	0.3	n	4.3	
198	1,122	1,188	0.40	2.0	13	0.3	3	5.0	
234	693	1,584	0.53	9.6	23	**0.8**	n	2.0	
497	784	1,190	0.32	2.8	**49**	0.4	0	0.6	
429	1,155	1,056	0.43	4.3	n	0.4	n	0.3	
180	225	1,080	0.48	2.1	11	0.3	9	1.5	
n	170	350	0.10	1.0	n	0.5	n	2.3	
58	66	330	0.10	0.8	n	n	n	n	
351	702	891	0.32	4.3	8	0.4	0	0.7	
64	117	485	0.06	1.2	n	n	n	0.1	
220	280	1,020	0.20	5.0	n	0.3	78	2.4	
980	**1,645**	2,065	0.42	6.3	25	0.5	1	0.6	

FISH AND FISH DISHES

FOOD	AVERAGE PORTION SIZE	TOTAL CALORIES	MINERALS	
	oz per portion	kcals per portion	Calcium (mg/portion) (QCT: 1000mg/day)	Magnesium (mg/portion) (QCT: 320mg/day)
White fish				
Cod, fried in batter	4	239	80	30
Cod, grilled	4	114	12	31
Haddock, fried	4	209	144	25
Plaice, fried in batter	4	308	88	24
Skate, fried in batter	4	202	60	32
Sole, flounder, steamed	4	109	25	24
Oily fish				
Anchovies, canned	½	29	45	8
Herring, grilled	4	217	95	50
Kipper, grilled	4	306	72	37
Mackerel, smoked	5	531	30	42
Salmon, canned	1 ¾	77	46	13
Salmon, grilled	3 ½	215	25	32
Salmon, smoked	1 ¾	71	10	16
Sardines, canned	3 ½	172	540	45
Sardines, in tomato sauce	1 ¾	72	125	15
Trout, grilled	4	162	25	31
Tuna, canned	3 ½	99	8	27
Seafood				
Lobster, boiled	3 ¼	93	56	31
Mussels, boiled	1 ½	42	21	15
Prawns/shrimp, boiled	2	59	66	29
Squid (calamare), fried in batter	2 ¼	127	53	15
Fish products and dishes				
Cod roe, fried	4	242	16	11
Fish sticks	2	143	51	13
Pasta with seafood	9	275	95	50
Taramasalata	1 ¾	252	11	3

	MINERALS			TRACE ELEMENTS				
Phosphorus (mg/portion) (QCT: 700mg/day)	Potassium (mg/portion) (QCT: 3500mg/day)	Sodium Chloride (mg/portion) (max: 3900mg/day)	Copper (mg/portion) (QCT: 0.9mg/day)	Iron (mg/portion) (QCT: 18mg/day)	Iodine (µg/portion) (QCT: 150µg/day)	Manganese (mg/portion) (QCT: 1.8mg/day)	Selenium (µg/portion) (QCT: 55µg/day)	Zinc (mg/portion) (QCT: 8mg/day)
240	348	192	0.05	0.6	n	0.1	n	0.6
240	456	109	0.05	0.1	156	tr	40	0.6
240	276	348	0.06	1.0	**300**	**0.3**	22	0.5
204	252	252	0.07	0.6	n	0.2	7	0.8
216	288	168	0.11	1.2	n	n	n	1.1
300	336	144	0.01	0.7	n	n	**88**	0.6
45	35	590	0.03	0.6	n	tr	n	0.5
372	**516**	192	0.23	1.9	46	0.1	55	1.4
312	468	**1,128**	0.17	2.2	76	0.1	43	1.3
315	465	1,125	0.14	1.8	150	tr	50	1,7
85	130	215	0.03	0.3	30	tr	13	0.4
300	430	54	0.04	0.5	44	tr	31	0.7
125	210	940	0.05	0.3	n	tr	12	0.2
510	320	530	0.16	2.3	23	0.2	41	2.3
140	155	145	0.08	1.3	32	0.1	15	0.4
300	492	66	0.06	0.5	18	tr	25	0.6
170	230	320	0.05	1.0	13	tr	78	0.7
234	234	297	**1.22**	0.7	90	tr	49	2.3
76	56	144	0.08	**2.7**	48	0.1	17	0.9
162	156	954	0.12	0.7	18	tr	14	1.3
104	150	57	0.34	0.5	12	0.1	23	0.6
360	204	144	0.26	1.2	n	0.1	n	**4.0**
132	156	270	0.02	0.5	72	0.1	13	0.2
250	475	425	0.18	1.0	98	**0.3**	30	1.3
25	30	325	n	0.2	n	0.1	n	0.2

DAIRY PRODUCTS

FOOD	AVERAGE PORTION SIZE	TOTAL CALORIES	MINERALS	
	oz/fl oz per portion	kcals per portion	Calcium (mg/portion) (QCI: 1000mg/day)	Magnesium (mg/portion) (QCI: 320mg/day)
Milk				
Skim milk	7	**64**	244	22
Semi-skim (low-fat) milk	7	**92**	240	22
Whole (full-fat) milk	7	**132**	236	22
Goat's milk	7	**124**	200	26
Soy milk, unsweetened	7	**52**	26	**30**
Milkshake, thick	7	**176**	258	26
Cream (2 tbs)				
Light cream	1	**58**	27	2
Heavy cream	1	**149**	15	2
Crème fraîche	1	**113**	17	2
Cheeses				
Brie/camembert	1 ½	**137**	102	6
Cheddar/Monterey Jack	1 ½	**166**	296	12
Cottage cheese	1 ½	**40**	51	5
Cream cheese	1 ½	**176**	39	4
Edam	1 ½	**136**	318	14
Feta	1 ½	**100**	144	8
Goat's cheese, soft	1 ½	**128**	53	6
Gouda	1 ½	**151**	309	13
Mozzarella, fresh	1 ½	**103**	145	6
Parmesan, fresh	1 ½	**166**	**410**	16
Stilton	1 ½	**164**	130	6
Strong blue	1 ½	**137**	195	8
Yogurt				
Full-fat yogurt, plain	5	**119**	300	29
Greek-style set yogurt, plain	5	**200**	189	20
Greek-style yogurt, sheep's milk	5	**138**	225	24
Soy yogurt, with fruit	5	**110**	21	23
Fromage frais, plain	3 ½	**113**	110	11

continues

	MINERALS			TRACE ELEMENTS					
Phosphorus (mg/portion) (QCT: 700mg/day)	Potassium (mg/portion) (QCT: 3500mg/day)	Sodium Chloride (mg/portion) (max: 3900mg/day)	Copper (mg/portion) (QCT: 0.9mg/day)	Iron (mg/portion) (QCT: 18mg/day)	Iodine (µg/portion) (QCT: 150µg/day)	Manganese (mg/portion) (QCT: 1.8mg/day)	Selenium (µg/portion) (QCT: 55µg/day)	Zinc (mg/portion) (QCT: 8mg/day)
192	320	88	tr	0.1	58	tr	2	1.0
188	312	86	tr	tr	60	tr	2	0.8
186	310	86	tr	0.1	62	tr	2	0.8
180	340	84	0.06	0.2	n	tr	n	1.0
96	148	64	0.18	0.9	2	**0.6**	8	0.6
240	342	114	tr	tr	74	tr	4	0.2
24	31	9	tr	tr	n	tr	n	0.1
16	20	7	tr	tr	11	tr	1	0.1
17	24	7	tr	tr	2	tr	0	0.1
93	36	222	tr	tr	6	tr	2	0.8
202	30	289	0.01	0.1	12	tr	2	1.6
68	64	120	tr	tr	10	tr	2	0.2
40	64	120	0.02	tr	n	tr	2	0.2
203	36	398	tr	0.1	5	tr	3	1.5
112	38	576	0.03	0.1	n	tr	2	0.4
92	53	240	0.02	tr	20	tr	2	0.4
199	33	370	tr	0.1	n	tr	3	1.6
107	20	158	tr	tr	7	tr	2	1.1
272	61	302	**0.34**	0.3	29	tr	5	**2.0**
126	38	315	0.02	0.1	16	tr	3	1.2
138	35	488	tr	tr	5	tr	3	1.2
255	**420**	120	tr	0.2	**95**	tr	3	1.1
207	276	99	tr	0.2	59	tr	5	0.8
210	285	225	tr	tr	n	tr	2	0.8
108	141	36	tr	0.8	15	0.3	3	0.3
123	143	36	0.03	0.1	17	tr	3	0.4

DAIRY PRODUCTS

FOOD	AVERAGE PORTION SIZE	TOTAL CALORIES	MINERALS	
	oz per portion	kcals per portion	Calcium (mg/portion) (QCT: 1000mg/day)	Magnesium (mg/portion) (QCI: 320mg/day)
Ice cream				
Dairy ice cream	3 ½	**215**	100	12
Non-dairy ice cream	3 ½	**153**	72	11
Eggs and egg dishes				
Egg, boiled	1 ¾	**74**	29	6
Egg, fried	2	**107**	39	8
Egg, scrambled	4	**308**	80	14
Omelet	4	**234**	61	14
Quiche	4	**378**	314	22

	MINERALS						TRACE ELEMENTS		
Phosphorus (mg/portion) (QCT: 700mg/day)	Potassium (mg/portion) (QCT: 3500mg/day)	Sodium Chloride (mg/portion) (max: 3900mg/day)	Copper (mg/portion) (QCT: 0.9mg/day)	Iron (mg/portion) (QCT: 18mg/day)	Iodine (µg/portion) (QCT: 150µg/day)	Manganese (mg/portion) (QCT: 1.8mg/day)	Selenium (µg/portion) (QCT: 55µg/day)	Zinc (mg/portion) (QCT: 8mg/day)
91	174	60	tr	tr	57	tr	2	0.3
74	164	62	tr	0.1	36	tr	2	0.2
100	65	70	0.04	1.0	27	tr	6	0.7
138	90	96	0.05	1.3	36	tr	7	0.9
182	164	266	0.08	1.9	65	tr	11	1.3
210	140	**1,229**	0.08	**2.0**	60	tr	**12**	1.3
272	149	439	0.07	1.2	n	tr	6	1.9

FATS AND OILS

FOOD	AVERAGE PORTION SIZE	TOTAL CALORIES	MINERALS	
(amounts in brackets represent size of average portion)	oz/fl oz per portion	kcals per portion	Calcium (mg/portion) (QCI: 1000mg/day)	Magnesium (mg/portion) (QCI: 320mg/day)
Cooking fats (1 tbs)				
Ghee, butter	½	135	tr	tr
Ghee, vegetable	½	134	tr	tr
Lard	½	134	tr	tr
Suet, beef	½	124	tr	tr
Suet, vegetable	½	125	tr	tr
Table fats (on 1 slice of bread)				
Butter	¼	74	tr	tr
Spread	¼	68	tr	tr
Low-fat spread	¼	39	tr	tr
Margarine, hard	¼	72	tr	tr
- hard vegetable	¼	74	tr	tr
- polyunsaturated	¼	75	tr	tr
Spread (70–80% fat)	¼	64	tr	tr
- (60% fat)	¼	55	tr	tr
- with olive oil	¼	57	tr	tr
- (35–40% fat)	¼	37	tr	tr
- (20–25% fat)	¼	25	tr	tr
Oils (1 tbs)				
Cod liver oil	½	135	tr	tr
Corn oil	½	135	tr	tr
Evening primrose oil	½	135	tr	tr
Grapeseed oil	½	135	tr	tr
Olive oil	½	135	tr	tr
Safflower oil	½	135	tr	tr
Sesame oil	½	135	tr	tr
Sunflower oil	½	135	tr	tr
Vegetable oil, blended	½	135	tr	tr
Walnut oil	½	135	tr	tr
Wheat germ oil	½	135	tr	tr

	MINERALS			TRACE ELEMENTS					
Phosphorus (mg/portion) (QCT: 700mg/day)	Potassium (mg/portion) (QCT: 3500mg/day)	Sodium Chloride (mg/portion) (max: 3900mg/day)	Copper (mg/portion) (QCT: 0.9mg/day)	Iron (mg/portion) (QCT: 18mg/day)	Iodine (µg/portion) (QCT: 150µg/day)	Manganese (mg/portion) (QCT: 1.8mg/day)	Selenium (µg/portion) (QCT: 55µg/day)	Zinc (mg/portion) (QCT: 8mg/day)
tr	tr	tr	tr	tr	n	tr	tr	tr
tr	tr	tr	**0.02**	tr	n	tr	tr	tr
tr	tr	tr	tr	tr	tr	tr	tr	tr
tr	tr	tr	tr	tr	1	tr	tr	tr
tr	tr	2	tr	tr	tr	tr	tr	tr
tr	tr	75	tr	tr	**4**	tr	tr	tr
tr	tr	67	tr	tr	n	tr	tr	tr
tr	tr	51	tr	tr	n	tr	tr	tr
tr	tr	**94**	tr	tr	n	tr	n	n
tr	tr	40	tr	tr	n	tr	n	n
tr	tr	68	tr	tr	n	tr	n	n
tr	tr	80	tr	tr	n	tr	n	n
tr	tr	71	tr	tr	n	tr	n	n
tr	tr	60	tr	tr	n	tr	n	n
tr	tr	65	tr	tr	n	tr	n	n
tr	tr	54	tr	tr	n	tr	n	n
tr	tr	tr	tr	tr	tr	tr	tr	tr
tr	tr	tr	tr	tr	tr	tr	tr	tr
tr	tr	tr	tr	tr	tr	tr	tr	tr
tr	tr	tr	tr	tr	tr	tr	tr	tr
tr	tr	tr	tr	tr	tr	tr	tr	tr
tr	tr	tr	tr	tr	tr	tr	tr	tr
tr	tr	tr	tr	tr	tr	tr	tr	tr
tr	tr	tr	tr	tr	tr	tr	tr	tr
tr	tr	tr	tr	tr	tr	tr	tr	tr
tr	tr	tr	tr	tr	tr	tr	tr	tr
tr	tr	tr	tr	tr	tr	tr	tr	tr

GRAINS, CEREALS, BREADS

FOOD	AVERAGE PORTION SIZE	TOTAL CALORIES	MINERALS	
	oz per portion	kcals per portion	Calcium (mg/portion) (QCT: 1000mg/day)	Magnesium (mg/portion) (QCT: 320mg/day)
Flours and grains				
Barley, pearl	3 ½	360	20	65
Buckwheat	3 ½	364	12	48
Bulgur wheat	3 ½	353	44	140
Cornstarch	3 ½	354	15	7
Couscous	3 ½	227	19	n
Custard powder	3 ½	354	15	7
Millet	3 ½	354	55	110
Oatmeal	3 ½	401	55	110
Quinoa	3 ½	309	79	210
Rice, brown	7	282	8	86
Rice, white	7	276	36	22
Rice flour	3 ½	366	24	23
Rye flour	3 ½	335	32	92
Soy flour	3 ½	447	210	240
Wheat flour, white	3 ½	341	140	20
Wheat flour, wholewheat	3 ½	310	38	120
Wheat germ	¾	76	14	30
Wheat bran	½	31	17	78
Noodles and pasta (cooked)				
Noodles, egg	10	186	15	24
Noodles, plain	10	186	15	24
Pasta, white	10	312	21	45
Pasta, wholewheat	10	339	33	126
Pastry				
Puff pastry	3 ½	373	58	12
Shortcrust pastry	3 ½	449	85	15
Breakfast cereals				
All-bran	1 ¾	126	35	185
Coco pops	1 ¾	193	18	n

continues

	MINERALS				TRACE ELEMENTS			
Phosphorus (mg/portion) (QCT: 700mg/day)	Potassium (mg/portion) (QCT: 3500mg/day)	Sodium Chloride (mg/portion) (max: 3900mg/day)	Copper (mg/portion) (QCT: 0.9mg/day)	Iron (mg/portion) (QCT: 18mg/day)	Iodine (µg/portion) (QCT: 150µg/day)	Manganese (mg/portion) (QCT: 1.8mg/day)	Selenium (µg/portion) (QCT: 55µg/day)	Zinc (mg/portion) (QCT: 8mg/day)
210	270	3	0.40	3.0	n	1.3	1	2.1
150	220	1	0.70	2.0	n	1.6	9	2.6
330	290	5	0.56	4.9	n	n	n	n
39	61	52	0.13	1.4	n	n	n	0.3
240	n	n	n	5.0	n	n	n	n
39	61	320	0.05	1.4	n	n	n	0.3
380	370	33	0.23	4.1	n	3.7	3	3.3
380	370	33	0.23	4.1	n	3.9	3	3.3
230	780	61	0.82	7.8	n	n	n	3.3
240	198	2	0.66	1.0	n	1.8	8	1.4
108	108	2	0.26	0.4	7	0.4	8	1.4
130	240	5	0.20	1.9	n	n	n	n
360	410	1	0.42	2.7	n	0.7	n	3.0
600	1,660	9	2.92	6.9	n	2.3	9	3.9
110	150	3	0.15	2.0	7	0.6	4	0.6
320	340	3	0.45	3.9	n	3.1	6	2.9
263	238	1	0.23	2.1	n	3.1	1	4.3
180	174	4	0.20	1.9	n	1.4	tr	2.4
93	69	45	0.18	0.9	n	0.5	n	0.9
84	39	3	0.18	0.9	tr	0.5	tr	0.9
132	72	tr	0.30	1.5	tr	0.8	tr	1.5
330	420	135	0.54	4.2	n	2.7	n	3.3
54	70	310	0.14	0.9	n	0.2	n	0.4
68	91	410	0.10	1.3	7	0.4	2	0.4
310	450	740	0.22	6.0	n	n	n	4.2
60	95	440	0.10	3.4	n	n	n	n

GRAINS, CEREALS, BREADS

FOOD	AVERAGE PORTION SIZE	TOTAL CALORIES	MINERALS	
(where appropriate, numbers in brackets represent number of items in average portion)	oz per portion	kcals per portion	Calcium (mg/portion) (QCT: 1000mg/day)	Magnesium (mg/portion) (QCT: 320mg/day)
Corn flakes	1 ¾	178	8	7
Fruit 'n' Fibre	1 ¾	176	26	n
Grapenuts	1 ¾	173	19	48
Muesli (Swiss style)	2 ½	255	84	60
Porridge (made with water)	7	98	14	36
Puffed wheat	1 ¾	161	13	70
Rice Krispies	1 ¾	185	10	25
Shredded wheat (2)	1 ¾	163	19	65
Special K	1 ¾	190	35	26
Weetabix (2)	1 ½	142	14	48
Breads and rolls				
Bagel (1)	3 ¼	246	5	31
Brown bread (1 slice)	1 ½	87	40	21
Chapati (1)	2	111	33	20
French stick (2 in slice)	1 ½	108	52	24
Granary bread (1 slice)	1 ½	94	31	45
Naan bread (1)	5 ½	538	256	44
Papadum (fried) (2)	¾	96	18	23
Pita bread (1 large)	3 ½	252	86	12
Rye bread (1 slice)	¾	55	20	22
Wheat germ bread (1 slice)	1 ½	105	48	10
White bread (1 slice)	1 ½	94	44	11
Wholewheat bread (1 slice)	1 ½	86	22	30
Croissant (1)	1 ¾	180	40	13
Hamburger bun (1)	1 ¾	132	65	16
Soft white roll (1)	1 ¾	135	70	17
Wholewheat roll (1)	1 ¾	121	28	35

	MINERALS			TRACE ELEMENTS				
Phosphorus (mg/portion) (QCT: 700mg/day)	Potassium (mg/portion) (QCT: 3500mg/day)	Sodium Chloride (mg/portion) (max: 3900mg/day)	Copper (mg/portion) (QCT: 0.9mg/day)	Iron (mg/portion) (QCT: 18mg/day)	Iodine (µg/portion) (QCT: 150µg/day)	Manganese (mg/portion) (QCT: 1.8mg/day)	Selenium (µg/portion) (QCT: 55µg/day)	Zinc (mg/portion) (QCT: 8mg/day)
19	50	555	0.02	3.4	3	tr	1	0.2
100	225	280	0.12	3.4	n	n	n	n
125	155	295	0.23	4.8	n	n	n	2.1
196	308	266	0.07	3.9	n	n	n	1.8
94	92	66	0.06	1.0	n	0.9	n	0.8
175	195	2	0.28	2.3	n	n	n	1.4
65	75	630	0.05	3.4	n	0.5	n	0.6
170	165	4	0.20	2.1	n	n	n	1.2
120	115	575	0.07	6.7	n	n	n	1.0
116	148	148	0.22	2.4	n	n	n	0.8
25	360	1	0.09	0.3	7	0.4	1	0.2
60	68	216	0.06	0.9	n	0.5	n	0.4
66	83	66	0.11	1.2	n	0.7	n	0.6
44	52	228	0.06	0.8	2	0.2	2	0.3
72	76	232	0.07	1.1	n	0.6	n	0.6
208	288	608	0.19	2.1	**20**	0.7	tr	1.3
65	195	637	0.13	2.9	n	0.3	n	0.7
87	105	494	0.20	1.6	n	0.4	n	0.6
40	48	145	0.05	0.6	n	0.3	n	0.3
72	76	228	0.08	1.2	6	0.7	n	0.8
36	44	208	0.08	0.6	2	0.2	2	0.2
80	92	220	0.10	1.1	tr	0.8	3	0.7
65	70	195	0.13	1.0	n	0.2	n	0.5
75	55	275	0.07	1.2	6	0.2	5	0.4
60	65	320	0.10	1.1	6	0.3	3	0.5
85	115	230	0.13	1.8	tr	0.8	4	0.8

BISCUITS, CAKES, DESSERTS

FOOD	AVERAGE PORTION SIZE	TOTAL CALORIES	MINERALS	
(where appropriate, numbers in brackets represent number of items in average portion)	oz per portion	kcals per portion	Calcium (mg/portion) (QCI: 1000mg/day)	Magnesium (mg/portion) (QCI: 320mg/day)
Biscuits and cookies				
Chocolate cookie (1)	³/₄	131	28	11
Cream cracker (1)	¹/₂	66	17	4
Crispbread, rye (1)	¹/₂	32	5	10
Flapjack (oatmeal cookie) (1)	2	290	22	29
Graham cracker (1)	¹/₂	71	14	3
Oatcake (1)	¹/₂	66	8	15
Plain cookie (1)	¹/₂	46	12	2
Plain cracker (1)	¹/₂	44	12	2
Shortbread (1)	¹/₂	75	14	2
Wholewheat cookie (1)	¹/₂	54	17	18
Wholewheat cracker (1)	¹/₂	62	17	7
Cakes				
Chocolate cake (1 slice)	2 ¹/₂	319	53	**32**
Fruit cake (1 slice)	2 ¹/₂	248	42	18
Gâteau (1 slice)	2 ¹/₂	236	42	6
Sponge cake (1 slice)	2 ¹/₂	321	46	6
Jelly roll (1 slice)	1 ¹/₄	97	34	4
Desserts				
Cheesecake (1 slice)	3 ³/₄	452	70	10
Christmas pudding	3 ¹/₂	291	79	27
Fruit crisp/cobbler	6	337	83	15
Custard sauce (made with milk)	5	176	**195**	20
Fruit pie	4	223	58	11
Pancake (1)	3 ³/₄	331	121	15
Rice pudding	7	178	186	22
Trifle	6	272	134	26
Buns and pastries				
Crumpet (1)	1 ¹/₂	71	44	6
Currant bun (1)	2	178	66	16

continues

	MINERALS						TRACE ELEMENTS		
Phosphorus (mg/portion) (QCT: 700mg/day)	Potassium (mg/portion) (QCT: 3500mg/day)	Sodium Chloride (mg/portion) (max: 3900mg/day)	Copper (mg/portion) (QCT: 0.9mg/day)	Iron (mg/portion) (QCT: 18mg/day)	Iodine (µg/portion) (QCT: 150µg/day)	Manganese (mg/portion) (QCT: 1.8mg/day)	Selenium (µg/portion) (QCT: 55µg/day)	Zinc (mg/portion) (QCT: 8mg/day)
---	---	---	---	---	---	---	---	---
33	58	40	0.06	0.4	n	n	n	0.2
17	18	92	0.03	0.3	2	0.1	1	0.1
31	50	22	0.04	0.4	2	0.4	tr	0.3
96	120	168	0.14	1.3	n	**1.2**	1	**0.9**
13	26	90	0.04	0.5	n	0.1	n	0.1
63	51	185	0.06	0.7	n	0.5	n	0.3
8	14	41	0.01	0.2	n	n	n	0.1
9	14	47	0.01	0.2	n	n	n	0.1
11	15	35	0.02	0.2	3	0.1	tr	0.1
51	59	71	0.06	0.5	n	0.4	7	0.4
26	30	105	0.04	0.4	n	0.2	n	0.2
147	133	301	**0.27**	1.3	24	0.1	4	0.8
77	273	175	0.18	1.2	**105**	n	n	0.4
66	62	39	0.04	0.6	12	0.1	n	0.4
105	57	245	0.07	0.8	18	0.1	4	0.5
63	39	46	0.04	0.5	9	n	3	0.2
105	121	341	0.12	1.0	n	0.1	n	0.7
76	350	200	0.22	1.5	n	0.4	7	0.5
56	323	116	0.17	1.0	10	0.3	2	0.3
165	255	122	tr	0.2	n	n	n	0.6
40	216	144	0.12	0.6	6	0.2	1	0.2
121	165	58	0.06	0.9	26	0.2	3	0.7
160	280	100	0.06	0.4	n	n	n	0.8
145	255	92	0.07	1.0	n	0.1	n	0.7
64	33	288	0.07	0.4	0	0.1	10	0.2
60	126	138	0.11	1.1	n	0.3	n	0.4

BISCUITS, CAKES, DESSERTS

FOOD	AVERAGE PORTION SIZE	TOTAL CALORIES	MINERALS	
(where appropriate, numbers in brackets represent number of items in average portion)	oz per portion	kcals per portion	Calcium (mg/portion) (QCI: 1000mg/day)	Magnesium (mg/portion) (QCI: 320mg/day)
Danish pastry (1)	3 ¾	**411**	101	26
Doughnut (jelly) (1)	2 ½	**252**	54	14
Greek pastry (Baklava) (1)	3 ½	**322**	44	22
Hot cross bun (1)	1 ¾	**155**	55	12
Muffin (American)	2 ½	**256**	39	25
Muffin (English) (1)	2 ½	**198**	98	20
Scone (1)	1-¾	**181**	90	9
Teacake (1)	2	**178**	53	17
Waffle (1)	2 ¼	**217**	169	14

	MINERALS							TRACE ELEMENTS	
Phosphorus (mg/portion) (QCI: 700mg/day)	Potassium (mg/portion) (QCI: 3500mg/day)	Sodium Chloride (mg/portion) (max: 3900mg/day)	Copper (mg/portion) (QCI: 0.9mg/day)	Iron (mg/portion) (QCI: 18mg/day)	Iodine (μg/portion) (QCI: 150μg/day)	Manganese (mg/portion) (QCI: 1.8mg/day)	Selenium (μg/portion) (QCI: 55μg/day)	Zinc (mg/portion) (QCI: 8mg/day)
---	---	---	---	---	---	---	---	---
108	187	209	0.07	1.4	n	0.4	n	0.6
53	83	135	0.07	0.9	18	0.2	n	0.4
70	90	310	0.14	0.9	n	0.3	n	0.4
55	100	60	0.12	0.8	n	0.2	n	0.4
46	**525**	11	0.21	0.7	4	0.1	1	0.4
105	126	91	0.14	1.3	n	0.3	**20**	0.6
230	75	**385**	0.10	0.7	10	0.2	1	0.4
60	132	162	0.14	**1.6**	n	0.3	n	0.4
241	124	377	0.07	0.9	22	0.2	3	0.5

SUGAR PRODUCTS

FOOD	AVERAGE PORTION SIZE	TOTAL CALORIES	MINERALS	
(where appropriate, numbers in brackets represent size of average portion)	oz per portion	kcals per portion	Calcium (mg/portion) (QCI: 1000mg/day)	Magnesium (mg/portion) (QCI: 320mg/day)
Sugars and syrups (1 tbs)				
Honey	½	58	tr	tr
Molasses	½	53	42	48
Sugar, brown	½	72	11	3
Sugar, white	½	79	tr	tr
Syrup, light corn	½	60	3	tr
Syrup, maple	½	52	13	3
Treacle, black	½	51	110	36
Preserves and spreads (1 tbs)				
Chocolate nut spread	½	110	9	10
Fruit spread	½	24	5	6
Jelly	½	52	16	9
Chocolate				
Chocolate bar	1 ¾	221	80	18
Milk chocolate	1 ¾	260	110	25
Plain chocolate	1 ¾	255	17	45
Confectionery				
Hard candy	1 ¾	164	3	1
Cereal crunchy bar	1 ¾	234	39	43
Fruit pastilles	1 ¾	164	14	3
Halva (with carrot)	1 ¾	177	75	10
Liquorice shapes	1 ¾	139	220	85
Nougat	1 ¾	192	13	12
Peppermints	1 ¾	197	4	2
Turkish delight (with nuts)	1 ¾	172	11	4

	MINERALS					TRACE ELEMENTS		
Phosphorus (mg/portion) (QCT: 700mg/day)	Potassium (mg/portion) (QCT: 3500mg/day)	Sodium Chloride (mg/portion) (max: 3900mg/day)	Copper (mg/portion) (QCT: 0.9mg/day)	Iron (mg/portion) (QCT: 18mg/day)	Iodine (µg/portion) (QCT: 150µg/day)	Manganese (mg/portion) (QCT: 1.8mg/day)	Selenium (µg/portion) (QCT: 55µg/day)	Zinc (mg/portion) (QCT:8mg/day)
3	10	2	0.01	0.1	tr	0.1	tr	0.2
6	292	7	0.10	0.9	tr	0.3	tr	0.1
tr	28	6	0.01	0.3	tr	tr	tr	tr
tr	tr	1	0.02	tr	tr	tr	tr	tr
tr	12	54	0.01	0.1	tr	tr	tr	tr
tr	40	2	0.01	0.2	tr	0.7	tr	0.8
6	352	36	0.16	4.3	tr	0.5	n	0.2
36	96	44	0.08	0.4	n	0.2	tr	0.4
15	60	85	0.03	0.3	1	0.1	tr	0.1
26	76	58	0.06	0.6	n	0.1	tr	0.2
75	125	75	0.16	0.6	n	0.2	1	0.6
110	195	43	0.12	0.7	**15**	0.1	**2**	0.6
70	150	3	**0.36**	1.2	2	0.3	**2**	0.7
6	tr	13	0.05	0.2	n	n	tr	n
145	180	37	0.15	1.3	n	1.1	n	**0.9**
tr	14	17	0.02	0.2	n	tr	tr	tr
65	185	50	0.04	0.3	9	0.1	1	0.3
37	**795**	**95**	**0.36**	**8.4**	n	**1.3**	n	0.5
37	120	60	0.11	0.4	n	0.1	1	0.3
tr	tr	5	0.02	0.1	n	n	tr	n
11	27	42	0.07	0.2	tr	tr	1	0.1

SOUPS AND SAUCES

FOOD	AVERAGE PORTION SIZE	TOTAL CALORIES	MINERALS	
	fl oz per portion	kcals per portion	Calcium (mg/portion) (QCT: 1000mg/day)	Magnesium (mg/portion) (QCT: 320mg/day)
Soups (1 cup)				
Bouillabaisse	9	338	113	35
Carrot and orange soup	9	50	33	5
Chicken soup	9	145	68	13
French onion soup	9	100	8	5
Gazpacho	9	113	28	20
Leek and potato soup	9	130	73	18
Lentil soup	9	293	40	50
Minestrone soup	9	158	35	18
Mushroom soup	9	115	75	10
Oxtail soup	9	110	100	15
Tomato soup	9	130	43	20
Vegetable soup	9	130	33	10
Sauces				
Black bean sauce	1	28	26	14
Brown sauce (spicy)	1	36	11	16
Curry sauce	4	90	35	21
Dressing, Thousand Island	1	97	7	3
Dressing, yogurt-based	1	88	17	2
Gravy (instant)	2 ½	24	tr	tr
Hollandaise sauce	2 ½	495	39	6
Mayonnaise	1	207	tr	tr
Mint sauce	½	10	12	5
Raita	1 ¾	29	75	9
Soy sauce	½	4	tr	4
Sweet and sour sauce	5	66	15	9
Tomato ketchup	1	35	4	6
Vinaigrette	1	139	n	n

	MINERALS				TRACE ELEMENTS			
Phosphorus (mg/portion) (QCT: 700mg/day)	Potassium (mg/portion) (QCT: 3500mg/day)	Sodium Chloride (mg/portion) (max: 3900mg/day)	Copper (mg/portion) (QCT: 0.9mg/day)	Iron (mg/portion) (QCT: 18mg/day)	Iodine (µg/portion) (QCT: 150µg/day)	Manganese (mg/portion) (QCT: 1.8mg/day)	Selenium (µg/portion) (QCT: 55µg/day)	Zinc (mg/portion) (QCT: 8mg/day)
400	**525**	135	0.13	1.8	n	0.1	n	1.0
25	213	375	0.03	0.5	3	0.1	tr	0.3
68	103	1,000	0.05	1.0	5	tr	tr	0.8
10	135	198	0.03	0.3	tr	tr	tr	tr
53	450	325	0.10	0.8	n	n	tr	0.3
88	400	208	0.05	1.0	10	0.2	3	0.5
200	**525**	225	**0.50**	**4.5**	n	n	n	**1.8**
70	300	350	0.13	1.3	n	**0.3**	n	0.5
75	138	**1,175**	0.10	0.8	8	tr	3	0.8
93	233	1,100	0.10	2.5	3	tr	tr	1.0
50	475	1,000	0.15	1.0	8	**0.3**	tr	0.5
50	275	325	0.05	0.8	n	0.2	3	0.3
25	45	753	0.06	1.7	n	0.2	n	0.2
6	99	450	0.03	0.4	n	0.1	n	0.1
36	207	1,127	0.06	1.3	n	0.2	n	0.2
10	39	270	0.02	0.1	2	tr	tr	0.1
18	36	195	tr	tr	n	tr	n	0.1
tr	tr	322	0.01	tr	n	tr	n	tr
105	44	700	0.06	1.6	**48**	0.1	**4**	0.8
8	tr	135	0.01	0.1	11	tr	n	tr
tr	21	69	0.03	0.7	tr	0.1	tr	tr
65	125	175	tr	0.1	22	0.1	tr	0.3
5	18	712	tr	0.2	n	tr	n	tr
15	140	585	0.03	0.8	n	**0.3**	n	0.2
9	105	489	0.02	0.1	n	tr	n	tr
n	n	138	n	n	n	n	n	n

PICKLES AND SAVOURIES

FOOD	AVERAGE PORTION SIZE	TOTAL CALORIES	MINERALS	
(where appropriate, numbers in brackets represent number of items in average portion)	oz per portion	kcals per portion	Calcium (mg/portion) (QCT: 1000mg/day)	Magnesium (mg/portion) (QCT: 320mg/day)
Pickles and chutneys				
Lime pickle	1 ½	71	48	32
Piccalilli	1 ½	34	6	2
Relish (corn/cucumber/onion)	1 ½	48	5	4
Sweet mango chutney	1 ½	76	4	8
Tomato chutney	1 ½	51	9	5
Tomatoes, sun-dried	1 ¾	248	16	14
Savoury snacks				
Breadsticks (grissini) (3)	¾	78	5	5
Popcorn, plain	1 ¾	297	5	41
Potato chips	1 ½	212	12	16
Potato chips, low-fat	1 ½	183	14	19
Pretzels	1 ¾	191	18	18
Tortilla chips	1 ¾	230	75	45

	MINERALS			TRACE ELEMENTS					
Phosphorus (mg/portion) (QCI: 700mg/day)	Potassium (mg/portion) (QCI: 3500mg/day)	Sodium Chloride (mg/portion) (max: 3900mg/day)	Copper (mg/portion) (QCI: 0.9mg/day)	Iron (mg/portion) (QCI: 18mg/day)	Iodine (µg/portion) (QCI: 150µg/day)	Manganese (mg/portion) (QCI: 1.8mg/day)	Selenium (µg/portion) (QCI: 55µg/day)	Zinc (mg/portion) (QCI: 8mg/day)	
n	96	212	0.08	**2.3**	n	n	n	0.1	
7	16	536	0.01	0.2	n	tr	n	tr	
10	44	136	0.03	0.1	n	tr	n	0.1	
3	17	520	tr	0.4	n	tr	n	tr	
13	116	52	0.04	0.4	1	0.1	tr	0.1	
23	230	500	**0.41**	1.0	**24**	0.1	tr	0.4	
22	32	172	0.02	0.2	n	0.1	n	0.1	
85	110	2	n	0.6	1	0.2	n	0.9	
44	376	336	0	0.6	n	0.1	n	0.2	
52	**408**	292	0.15	0.7	n	0.2	n	0.4	
55	75	**860**	0.13	2.2	n	**0.9**	n	0.5	
120	110	430	0.05	0.8	n	0.2	n	0.6	

DRINKS

FOOD	AVERAGE PORTION SIZE	TOTAL CALORIES	MINERALS	
(where appropriate, numbers in brackets represent size of average portion)	fl oz per portion	kcals per portion	Calcium (mg/portion) (QCT: 1000mg/day)	Magnesium (mg/portion) (QCT: 320mg/day)
Fruit juices (unsweetened)				
Apple juice	7	76	14	10
Cranberry juice	7	122	110	70
Grape juice	7	92	38	14
Grapefruit juice	7	66	28	16
Lemon juice (2 tsp)	¾	1	tr	1
Lime juice (2 tsp)	¾	2	tr	1
Mango juice	7	78	4	n
Orange juice	7	66	24	24
Passionfruit juice	7	94	14	58
Pineapple juice	7	82	16	12
Pomegranate juice	7	88	6	6
Prune juice	7	114	28	22
Hot drinks				
Coffee, black	7	4	6	15
Coffee, with milk	7	13	29	15
Coffee, Irish	7	160	21	11
Drinking chocolate (for 1 mug)	½	66	6	27
Tea, black	7	tr	tr	4
Tea, with milk	7	15	25	6
Tea, green	7	tr	4	tr
Tea, herbal	7	2	4	2
Soft drinks (carbonated)				
Cola	11	129	20	3
Fruit juice drink	11	129	23	23
Ginger beer	9	38	n	n
Lemonade	7	44	10	2
Sports drinks	7	120	14	14
Tonic water	9	83	3	0

continues

	MINERALS			TRACE ELEMENTS					
Phosphorus (mg/portion) (QCT: 700mg/day)	Potassium (mg/portion) (QCT: 3500mg/day)	Sodium Chloride (mg/portion) (max: 3900mg/day)	Copper (mg/portion) (QCT: 0.9mg/day)	Iron (mg/portion) (QCT: 18mg/day)	Iodine (µg/portion) (QCT: 150µg/day)	Manganese (mg/portion) (QCT: 1.8mg/day)	Selenium (µg/portion) (QCT: 55µg/day)	Zinc (mg/portion) (QCT: 8mg/day)
12	220	4	tr	0.2	tr	tr	tr	tr
130	**1,500**	30	**0.60**	2.0	**10**	0.4	**4**	1.0
28	110	14	tr	1.8	n	0.2	2	0.2
22	200	14	0.02	0.4	n	0.4	2	tr
tr	26	tr	0.01	tr	n	tr	0	tr
tr	22	tr	0.01	tr	n	tr	n	0
44	36	18	n	**3.0**	n	n	n	n
44	360	4	tr	0.6	4	0.2	2	tr
42	400	38	n	1.0	n	n	n	**1.6**
tr	106	16	0.04	0.4	tr	**1.4**	tr	0.2
16	400	2	0.14	0.4	n	n	n	n
38	420	24	0.08	1.4	6	0.2	tr	0.4
13	175	tr	tr	0.2	tr	0.1	tr	tr
30	184	11	tr	0.2	4	0.1	tr	0.2
25	137	11	tr	0.2	tr	0.1	tr	0.2
34	74	45	0.20	0.4	n	n	n	0.3
4	51	tr	0.02	tr	tr	0.3	tr	tr
23	76	11	0.02	0	n	0.3	tr	0.2
tr	38	2	tr	0.2	tr	tr	tr	tr
tr	17	tr	0.04	0.2	tr	0.1	tr	tr
99	3	17	tr	tr	tr	tr	tr	tr
7	89	26	tr	tr	tr	tr	tr	tr
n	n	n	n	n	tr	tr	tr	n
tr	30	14	tr	tr	tr	tr	tr	tr
4	54	16	tr	tr	tr	tr	tr	tr
0	0	10	tr	tr	tr	tr	tr	tr

DRINKS

FOOD	AVERAGE PORTION SIZE	TOTAL CALORIES	MINERALS	
	fl oz per portion	kcals per portion	Calcium (mg/portion) (QCT: 1000mg/day)	Magnesium (mg/portion) (QCT: 320mg/day)
Soft drinks (uncarbonated)				
Barley water (diluted)	7	28	tr	tr
Fruit juice drink (diluted)	7	60	tr	tr
Rosehip syrup (diluted)	7	92	n	n
Alcoholic drinks				
Beer, dark	10	177	24	21
Beer, lager	10	384	15	21
Beer, shandy	10	48	24	3
Beer, stout (eg. Guinness)	10	156	12	24
Cider	10	108	24	9
Champagne	4 1/2	95	4	8
Red wine	4 1/2	85	9	14
White wine	4 1/2	83	11	10
Port	2	79	tr	6
Sherry	2	58	4	7
Vermouth/martini	2	55	4	3
Cream liqueurs (eg. Kahlua)	3/4	81	5	tr
Liqueurs, high-strength (eg. Grand Marnier)	3/4	79	tr	tr
Liqueurs, med.-strength (eg. campari)	3/4	66	tr	tr
Spirits (eg. brandy/gin/whiskey)	3/4	56	tr	tr

	MINERALS			TRACE ELEMENTS					
Phosphorus (mg/portion) (QCT: 700mg/day)	Potassium (mg/portion) (QCT: 3500mg/day)	Sodium Chloride (mg/portion) (max: 3900mg/day)	Copper (mg/portion) (QCT: 0.9mg/day)	Iron (mg/portion) (QCT: 18mg/day)	Iodine (µg/portion) (QCT: 150µg/day)	Manganese (mg/portion) (QCT: 1.8mg/day)	Selenium (µg/portion) (QCT: 55µg/day)	Zinc (mg/portion) (QCT: 8mg/day)
tr	10	6	0	0	tr	0	0	0
tr	24	4	tr	tr	0	0	0	tr
n	10	**112**	n	n	0	n	0	n
42	96	18	0.03	0.3	tr	0.1	tr	0.3
57	117	21	tr	tr	tr	tr	tr	tr
15	18	21	tr	tr	tr	tr	tr	tr
78	144	18	tr	0.6	tr	tr	tr	tr
9	216	21	0.12	1.5	n	tr	tr	tr
9	71	5	0.01	0.6	n	tr	tr	tr
16	138	9	0.08	1.1	n	0.1	tr	0.1
8	76	5	0.01	0.6	n	0.1	tr	tr
6	49	2	0.05	0.2	n	tr	tr	tr
6	29	5	0.02	0.2	n	tr	tr	tr
3	17	6	0.02	0.2	n	tr	tr	tr
10	tr	22	tr	tr	n	tr	tr	0.1
tr	tr	2	tr	tr	n	tr	tr	tr
tr	tr	3	tr	tr	n	tr	n	tr
tr	tr	tr	tr	tr	tr	tr	tr	tr

Part 4
DIETS

In this part we explore a range of strategies for achieving weight loss. We begin by looking at the importance of exercise and good nutrition for achieving sustained weight loss. This is followed by a review of a range of popular diets, including calorie-controlled diets, high-protein diets, low-fat diets, and high-fat/low-carbohydrate diets. Next we are given some general principles for healthy slimming, and asked to consider the emotional triggers for over-eating. An "all-purpose" slimming plan provides a concrete example of how we can incorporate the principles of healthy dieting into our daily life. Then a 10-day detox and elimination diet takes us through the process of cutting out different foods, and then gradually reintroducing them. This enables us to find out which foods disagree with us.

Diets and dieting

The National Weight Control Registry (NWCR)—a national database of American individuals who have achieved successful weight loss—contains information on 2800 Americans over the age of 18 who have managed to maintain a 30 lb weight loss for a year or more. 55 per cent of those registered had participated in formal weight-loss programs; 20 per cent had used low-calorie liquid diets; 4.3 per cent had used weight-loss medications; and 1.3 per cent had undergone gastric bypass surgery. Almost all had previously tried several weight-loss methods without success. Of those who were successful, 61 per cent followed a more rigorous diet than before, and 81 per cent exercised more. The average successful slimmer expended about 2800 kcal per week on exercise (about one hour a day). This evidence confirms that diet without exercise rarely produces lasting weight loss, and suggests that structured programs make the process of dieting more effective.

As the majority of people wishing to lose weight also want to improve their long-term health, it is vital that slimming regimes incorporate the principles of healthy eating. Good nutrition is now accepted worldwide as the most powerful and cost-effective way of enhancing health and vitality, and of avoiding serious illness in the long term. A well-nourished body is better able to support and sustain weight loss than one fighting the effects of a poor diet.

Before looking at ways to make your slimming diet as healthy and effective as possible, here is a brief review of some popular weight-loss methods.

CALORIE-CONTROLLED DIETS

Calorie-controlled diets that restrict calorie intake to a daily maximum can certainly help us lose weight, but they also produce cravings— not only for more calories, but also for necessary nourishment. As it is not easy for us to distinguish between these two, we often find ourselves grabbing an illicit candy bar to provide some instant energy and a sense of relief and satisfaction.

Unfortunately, this satisfaction is often followed half an hour later by a headache and yet more cravings ... .

When calorie intake is restricted, the body changes its metabolism so that energy is provided from the burning up of fat stores. The change-over period lasts a few days and is usually accompanied by cravings, hunger, headaches, and low energy levels. When we fast these symptoms are soon replaced by increased energy levels and heightened well-being. However, calorie-controlled diets tend to leave the body stuck in the change-over state, constantly craving food and feeling unwell.

HIGH-PROTEIN DIETS

In an attempt to avoid the negative effects of calorie control, some slimming diets advocate a very high protein intake. This is because the level of protein in the blood controls the brain's hunger-center, so eating a protein-rich diet means you need to eat fewer calories to feel satisfied.

The downside is that a high-protein diet over a long period can cause quite severe health problems. This is because it may lack essential nutrients, phytochemicals, and fiber and, more importantly, because the body has no way of storing the protein it doesn't need. Any excess is excreted and may cause kidney problems, so if you decide to follow a high-protein slimming regime, remember to drink plenty of water (at least 3½ pints a day), and make sure that whatever carbohydrate you do eat comes from fresh plant foods that are high in fiber. If you intend to diet for an extended period, you should consult a qualified medical practitioner beforehand to ensure that you don't achieve weight loss at the expense of poor nutrition.

LOW-FAT DIETS

There is considerable debate about the role of excess dietary fat in the development of obesity, but it is clear from epidemiological studies that there is a worldwide association between high dietary fat intake and obesity. Laboratory studies on humans also show that individuals with access to high-fat foods will always eat these in preference to low-fat foods if given the choice, and that excess dietary fat is stored in the body with greater efficiency than excess dietary carbohydrate or protein. Diets designed to achieve weight loss by restricting fat intake have met with limited success, however. This may be because the body uses energy more efficiently when less is available.

HIGH-FAT/LOW-CARBOHYDRATE DIETS

As with high-protein diets, high-fat/low-carbohydrate diets can also reduce cravings because fats are calorie-dense, providing over twice as many calories of energy as carbohydrates and protein for the same weight—which makes it possible to feel satisfied with smaller portions. Advocates of the "eat fat, grow slim" approach claim that fat is the least fattening of all foods because, when carbohydrate intake is restricted, eating more fat turns up the metabolic thermostat, mobilizing fat stores and burning up the food we eat more efficiently. Based on the idea that humans evolved as predators with a diet naturally high in fat and protein, high-fat enthusiasts claim that the degeneration of health (and the human condition) in modern times is due to the shift toward a diet based on "useless" carbohydrate fuel, such as cereals and grains.

Although high-fat "stone age" diets have undoubtedly helped some people to lose weight, the balance of evidence suggests that most people would gain substantially more in health terms by increasing their intake of fresh fruits and vegetables, and moderating their intake of saturated fat.

GETTING THE MOST OUT OF YOUR SLIMMING DIET

Whatever type of slimming program you choose, there are a number of nutritional and lifestyle guidelines that will help to ensure that your diet is as healthy and effective as possible:

- **Eat a balanced diet.** From a nutritional perspective, the best diet is high in complex carbohydrates (60–65 per cent), fiber and simple fruit sugars, and contains no refined sugar at all. It provides a moderate amount of protein (10–15 per cent), a controlled amount of unsaturated fat (20–30 per cent), and very little saturated fat.

- **Eat fresh fruits and vegetables.** The easiest way to improve your diet is to greatly increase your fruit and vegetable intake and cut out dairy products altogether. (There are plenty of non-dairy alternatives on the market including soy, rice, oat and almond milks, nut butters and pure vegetable margarines.)

- **Eat more fiber.** Fiber and complex carbohydrates are crucial for slimming because they are low in calories and yet give a feeling of fullness. They also improve fat and cholesterol metabolism, and aid digestion.

- **Eat proper meals.** To achieve weight loss it is better to eat proper meals than snacks. If you need to snack, eat natural wholefoods, such as wholewheat sugar-free crackers, sugar-free cereal bars, carrot or celery sticks, bananas, papaya (paw-paw), apples, and sugar-free dried fruits.

- **Pay attention to the quality of the fats you eat.** Cut down dairy and animal fat in your diet to a minimum and use olive oil (or other cold-pressed vegetable oils) for cooking. Avoid sources of saturated fats, such as lard, fatty meats, cream, cheese, butter, and full-fat dairy products.

- **Drink plenty of water**—your body loses about 4–4$\frac{1}{2}$ pints of water each day (depending on activity level and climate) in sweat, urine, feces, and breathing.

- **Stay off alcoholic beverages and sugary hot or cold drinks.** Exchange these for water, fruit juices, herb teas, and chicory, dandelion or barley "coffees."

- **Start each meal with some fresh seasonal fruit.**

- **As far as possible, cut out all red and processed meats.** Steaks, burgers, and sausages tend to be high in both total fat and saturated fat. Eat more seafood, poultry, and pulses.

- **Beware of empty calories.** Avoid refined carbohydrates (such as added sugar, confectionery, cookies, and candy), alcohol, and processed snacks.

- **Read labels**—don't eat anything you don't agree with.

- **Eat papaya (paw-paw) or grapefruit every day.** Both contain phytochemicals which complement the action of pancreatic digestive enzymes. Eating them can help you to decrease your calorie intake by making better use of the food you do eat.

- **Exchange black tea and coffee for green tea.** Green tea contains methylxanthines and antioxidants, which boost metabolism and immunity.

- **Add dandelion to your diet.** Dandelion root enhances fat digestion and is a traditional weight-loss remedy. The fresh root can be cooked like parsnip or stir-fried, and there are a number of roasted dandelion root "coffees" available in health stores. Dandelion leaves can be added to fresh salads.

- **Include potatoes in your diet.** Potatoes contain a protein that stimulates the release of a chemical called cholecystokinin (CCK). In the brain, CCK acts as a satiety factor, signaling to the body that it has had enough to eat.

• **Take daily exercise.** Fat-burning is most efficient at around 50 per cent of maximum exercise capacity, so if you are not used to exercising, a 20–30 minute walk each day is a good start. Try to establish a daily routine, but have one day off each week. Cycling, dancing, fitness training, swimming, running, and stretching can all help to ensure that you make proper use of the food you eat. Obese individuals who achieve cardio-respiratory fitness have a lower mortality risk than sedentary people of normal weight, so even if weight loss is slow, exercise will do you good. Couch potatoes are jeopardizing their health, no matter how much they weigh.

• **Have breaks.** Rest is important for efficient digestion, so spend 15–30 minutes each day on relaxation or meditation. Taking short relaxation breaks during the day also decreases the need for snacks to keep brain and body going.

• **Get fresh air whenever you can** and use it as an alternative to stimulants, such as chocolate, tea, and coffee, to give you extra calorie-free energy.

DIET AND EMOTION

Eating satisfies the emotions as well as the stomach. The feelings of security and satisfaction that come from food can be traced back to infancy. Babies get very upset when they are hungry, and are easily calmed with food or by the sensation of eating (such as sucking a pacifier or a finger).

All forms of stress, anxiety, and fear eat up blood sugar and encourage us to reach for easy energy-fixes, such as candy, cakes, and snacks. Chronic stress is often soothed by thinking about, tasting, chewing, and digesting food, and such patterns can be very resistant to change. Managing stress and paying attention to your emotional needs are therefore an integral part of successful weight loss. It is also important to understand the extent to which emotional factors influence your diet and eating habits, to ensure that you can maintain a healthy weight when the dieting is over.

Diet Plans

ALL PURPOSE SLIMMING DIET

When losing weight, it is important to eat foods that are low in calories, yet high in vitamins, minerals, trace elements, essential fatty acids, and amino acids. It is also important to avoid stimulants (such as coffee, tea, chocolate, and sugar). Dairy products, apart from live yogurt, are also best avoided. Follow the daily plan below to get started, and improvize using your own favorite quality calorie choices.

DAILY PLAN

ON RISING
• Drink a glass of water or unsweetened fruit juice.

BREAKFAST
• Drink a cup of herb tea, green tea, fruit juice, or water.
• Eat half a grapefruit, followed by as much as you like of one of the following:
    - Fruit salad with added nuts and seeds.
    - Porridge with soy, rice, or almond milk.
    - Low-fat live yogurt or soy yogurt with dried fruits (soaked overnight) and a few nuts and seeds sprinkled over the top.
    - Fruit followed by wholewheat bread with honey or yeast extract.

MID-MORNING
• Drink one glass of water or fruit juice, or a cup of herb tea.
• If you need a snack, eat some pieces of fruit or some raw vegetable sticks

with oatcakes, crispbread, or rice cakes topped with nut butter or
low-fat spread.

LUNCH
• Eat at least two pieces of seasonal fruit; then a large plate of mixed salad
with herbs (for example, thyme, parsley, watercress, oregano), dressed with
vinaigrette and accompanied by wholewheat bread, rice cakes, oatcakes, or rye
bread, spread with houmous or nut butter.

MID-AFTERNOON
• Drink one glass of water or fruit juice, or a cup of herb tea.
• If you feel hungry, eat some sticks of raw carrot, cucumber, or celery, or some
pieces of fruit, together with rice cakes, crackers, or oatcakes.

EVENING MEAL
• Eat two pieces of seasonal fruit, followed by a portion of soup and a plate of
food comprising one half green vegetables, one third root vegetables and/or
grains, and one sixth fat and protein foods (see food groups below).

MID-EVENING
• Drink a cup of herb tea or a glass of water.

FRESH VEGETABLES: artichoke; asparagus; bean sprouts; beet greens; broccoli;
brussels sprouts; cabbage; cauliflower; celery; chicory; cress; cucumber; curly
kale; eggplant; fennel; green beans; leeks; lettuce; okra; onion; peas; peppers;
pumpkin; spinach; tomato; zucchini.

ROOT VEGETABLES AND GRAINS: beet; bulgur wheat; carrot; celeriac;
cereals; couscous; parsnip; potato; rutabaga; sweetcorn; sweet potato; turnip;
wholewheat bread; wholewheat pasta; wholegrain rice; wild rice.

FAT AND PROTEIN FOODS: avocado; dried beans; cheese; chick peas; crab;
egg; fish; lean meat (including chicken and ham); lentils; mushrooms; nuts
and seeds; olives; prawns or shrimp; tempeh; tofu.

DETOX AND ELIMINATION

The best times to detox are spring and autumn. Carry it out at a time when you can take things easy. Don't be surprised or unnerved if you feel a little nauseous or headachy at first. When you detox, the waste products and toxins your body has stored in fat tissue are cleared away. The higher levels of toxins in your blood during this process can make you feel unwell. Don't lose heart—the symptoms will soon pass, leaving you feeling, lighter, more awake, and more energetic than before. This diet involves gradually cutting certain drinks and foods out of your normal diet until you are drinking only water and grape juice. This is followed by the gradual reintroduction of different foods, one at a time, allowing you to see which ones agree with you and which do not.

10-DAY DETOX AND ELIMINATION

DAY 1

Eat normally but cut out tea, coffee, chocolate, alcohol, tobacco, and fizzy drinks. Replace these with green tea, herb tea, fruit juice, and plenty of water.

DAY 2

Cut out everything containing sugar. Replace these with fresh and dried fruit and nuts. Drink plenty of water

DAY 3

Cut out all meat and dairy products. If you are uncertain what to replace them with, try the following: for breakfast, the juice of one ruby-red grapefruit and muesli, or porridge with dried fruits and nuts, served with soy, rice, or almond milk; for lunch, mixed tofu and vegetable stir-fry, or mixed salad with rice; for an afternoon snack, fresh vegetable juice and fresh or dried fruit and nuts; for an aperitif, fresh vegetable juice; and for dinner, steamed vegetables and rice. Supplement these dishes with plenty of water between meals.

DAY 4

Cut out bread, rice, nuts, and other grains. Eat plenty of fresh fruit and vegetables (raw or steamed). Drink plenty of unsweetened fruit juice and water.

DAY 5

Eat fruit only. Consume as much as you like (particularly grapes), whenever you like. Drink plenty of unsweetened fruit juice and water.

DAY 6

Drink only grape juice and plenty of water.

DAY 7

Eat fruit only. Consume as much as you like (particularly grapes), whenever you like. Drink plenty of unsweetened fruit juice and water.

DAY 8

Eat plenty of fresh fruit and vegetables (raw or steamed). Drink lots of unsweetened fruit juice and water.

DAY 9

Reintroduce grains, bread, rice, and nuts. Eat lots of fresh fruit and vegetables, and drink plenty of unsweetened fruit juice and water.

DAY 10

Gently begin reintroducing your normal diet. Add one food type per day. Notice whether you experience any adverse reactions to particular items as you reintroduce them. If so, you may choose to cut these out of your diet altogether or at least limit your intake of them.

(Above all, after finishing your detox diet, don't rush out immediately for a big meal with wine and coffee—it could make you feel extremely unwell.)

Index